MOVING MOUNTAINS

A HERO'S JOURNEY

AUDRA RENE WEEKS

Editor: Vicki Neil
Cover Design: Heather Bednorz Design
Interior Layout: Soumi Goswami

This is a work of nonfiction based on the life and recollections of Audra Rene Weeks. Names and identifying details may have been withheld or altered to maintain anonymity. The author will not be held liable or responsible to any person or entity with respect to alleged damages caused directly or indirectly by the information in this book.

Audra Rene Weeks
www.audrareneweeks.com

MOVING MOUNTAINS

A HERO'S JOURNEY

AUDRA RENE WEEKS

Goodyear, AZ

For my children, Amber, Dylan, and Chandler.
Thank you for being my top three reasons why.
And
For all of those who have been through
a lot and are trying to heal.

CONTENTS

FORWARD

Audra. She came, she saw, she conquered. This beautiful redhead – poised, confident, and full of life. She CAME to me with so much to give to others. An energy and wisdom that radiated from head to toe. I felt it from the beginning. She didn't. You see, she had an internal dialogue that told her the opposite. One that came from her experiences. She was injured internally due to the impact of trauma. Her life was not like mine, nor yours. She had been through horrifying encounters that would destroy most human beings. Yet she was strong enough to keep on living.

When she came to me, she was ready to SEE from the inside out by working through her trauma. Trauma impacts us on a level that is difficult to comprehend. When trauma is left unresolved, our brains interpret sensory information coming in as a never-ending threat. We have no choice but to adapt to that threat in our thoughts, feelings, and behaviors. Our thoughts constantly remind us that the world is unsafe, nobody can be trusted, we have no power and control, we are not worth anything, and nobody will ever love us. Our emotions are a result of our thoughts – sad, scared, and angry. When we think and feel this way, our behaviors serve to protect us. We are now in fight, flight, or freeze.

When she came to me, she was in this self-protection mode and ready to change. She had hope that life was better than what she was living and that she deserved more. She worked from the inside out.

Her traumas were written from start to finish and the impact felt was translated to core beliefs. She challenged her core beliefs through cognitive reframing, and then she was ready to shatter them. As she shattered them, she reunited with her true self. She CONQUERED and is ready to live her best life!

Audra. She came, she saw, she conquered. This beautiful redhead CAME feeling broken but with an open mind and soul, ready for transformation; SAW the impact of her traumas on her life and experienced her emotions naturally; CONQUERED by shattering her mistaken beliefs viewing her past, present and future through different lenses. All the while, her energy, and wisdom permeated the surroundings, leaving a feeling of peace each time she came and left.

Mireya Roe, MA
Licensed Professional Counselor
Trauma Specialist

She will walk bravely into the test diving deep into the well of wisdom and knowledge that has brought her this far. And not just because she has learned many things, but because she has lived many things, and now she has the strength and courage to give it her all, press on toward the goal, and achieve the impossible.

For she is guided, and by grace, she can do this.

~ Morgan Harper Nichols

I WANT YOU TO KNOW

I genuinely think writing this book is something I came into this life to do. I also think it's a big reason why I have experienced all the things I've been through. You see, I believe that my healing is your healing and that your healing is my healing. There is no separation between us. I see that history repeats itself on an individual level and on a planetary level. I believe that in order to change this, healing and holding space for others to heal is crucial. When we do our own individual work, not only are we healing ourselves from the inside out, but we are also healing the collective as a whole. We are literally rewriting the Program of this current reality and releasing the weights that hold us all back from evolving.

Maybe writing this book and sharing my journey is some of my part in aiding to create this new reality. Maybe I had been given all these mountains to show others that they can be moved. Is this my opportunity to lead by example or perhaps even light the way for someone else? I want to show my beloved human family that they are not alone in their beautiful mess. I can only do my inner work, speak my truth, and hope.

This is my life. These are my experiences. These are my memories, my thoughts, and my feelings given to the best of my knowledge and my ability. This is a culmination of events that have greatly aided in the creation of the woman who is presented before you right now. This is my journey. These are my triumphs, my stumblings, my greatest fears, and my greatest joys come to life. So much painful and joyous growth!

I genuinely want to be of service to my human family 'out of love'. I believe that by sharing my own story, I can help so many other people, in many ways and on many levels. In this service, I hope to empower others, and add meaning to my own life.

I have come to realize that writing my story is going to take an astounding amount of courage. Reliving these events will require me to embrace diving deep into the dark places of my soul; only in this way can I be fully authentic.

And then there is the huge risk of exposing this darkness. What if others read my story and deem my journey unsuccessful? What happens to my life's meaning?

Of course, I know these fears are baseless. But the tremendous amount of emotional charge around them is inescapable. However, the truth is that if this book touches even one soul beyond my own, it's a success.

This is my life. Perhaps like yours, it is full of metaphors, irony, learning, growth, joy, and pain. But most of all, it's full of hope and love. Along the way and through my hero's journey and healing work, I've been learning how to love myself. I find it interesting how much we are taught in life, but we are never taught how to love ourselves. We have had to figure that out on our own. We have to unlearn and strip away who we were told and taught to be, and in that nakedness, find out who we truly are. Are we then, perhaps, someone who does not represent worth by the measures of what we were taught? It is in this moment that our opportunity lies to rise above what the world has taught us, and love the bare human and naked soul that's left standing there regardless.

I believe things are changing though. I think we, as a society, are doing a better job teaching our children and others how to love themselves. When others see us show up and expose our vulnerabilities, shining the light into our own darkness, and embarking on our hero's journey to move our mountains, they are seeing us get real. They bear witness to the struggle we endure to love ourselves and to accept ourselves as is. They watch us fight through our own self-created hell and finally step into the heavens of self-love. Our battle shows them the way; hopefully, they are spared the pain of our journey. In our own evolution, we are giving them permission to do the same.

Two AM and I'm still awake writing a song.
If I get it all down on paper, it's no longer inside of me,
threatening the life it belongs to.

And I feel like I'm naked in front of the crowd,
cause these words are my diary screaming out loud,
and I know that you'll use them however you want to.

But you can't jump the track.
We're like cars on a cable.
And life's like an hourglass glued to the table.

When no one can find the rewind button.
Now sing it if you understand.
And breathe......... Just breathe.

~ Anna Nalick, "Breathe"

CHAPTER 1

MY MOUNTAINS

We aren't made to live in the shadow of daunting haunting mountains. We were made to move them.

~Elizabeth Griffin

When I was 7 years old, one of my brothers was in a
life-altering accident.

~

When I was 8, that brother committed a violent suicide.

~

Right around the time I turned 14, my stepfather told me
of his desire to molest me.

~

When I was a junior in high school, he actually tried to.

~

When I was 17 years old, a peer raped me
while I was unconscious.

~

When I was barely 20, an uncle attempted to murder
me in my sleep because I was in the way.

CHAPTER 2

THE BACKGROUND MUSIC

ECHO

I am a woman who recognizes her own depth.
The Divinity of my architecture is not just limited to flesh and bone,
the femininity of my curve, the sacred geometry of my vibration, the
light of my auric flame.
I am a woman sculpted by the hands of
the Infinite Intelligence.
The entirety of the Universe is fashioned inside of me.

I AM THE ECHO OF GOD.

~S. Ajna

It's crazy to think that there are literally thousands, if not more, versions of ourselves out there in the world. We think that everyone sees the same "me", but we are interpreted differently by everyone we meet. This may seem like a far-fetched or perhaps even an overwhelming thought to you. But if you take a minute and think about it, every person that encounters us has a different view or perspective of who we are or who they think we are. They, through their own filters and life experiences, see us and experience us in a very unique and individual way. Because of this, no two people will ever have the same experience with us, nor will they see us exactly the same as someone else does, or even as we see ourselves for that matter. I find that absolutely fascinating.

⌒

Before I dive into the heart of the matter of this book, I probably should tell you a little bit about me. You know, provide a little background music if you will. This is a very brief overview of myself and some of my life, through my filters and my lenses. This is a little of who I think I am, some of what's important to me, and how I came to write this book.

My name is Audra. Currently, I am 46 years old. I was born and raised here in Phoenix, Arizona. I am the youngest of 7 kids. I know, that's a lot of kids! I have 5 half brothers and 1 half-sister.

I remember my twin brothers the most. I think it's because we were the closest in age. I got picked on a lot! Especially by one of the twins in particular, "J". I don't think it's an exaggeration when I say that I think he told me daily how ugly he thought I was. I am a freckle-faced redhead and, for whatever reason, when I was younger, those features were the ones he targeted. Not just by him either. It was within my peers as well. When I hit 5th and 6th grade, I got pretty chunky too, so being fat became another attribute that was targeted. In my memory, it seems as though the taunting was endless.

Today, J and I get along great; this teasing behavior is not part of his personality. Maybe this mean streak 40 plus years ago was the result of being picked on by our older brothers and this was a ripple effect. Or maybe he needed to feel as though he had some power in our rather chaotic household. Wherever this tendency came from, it's gone now.

Unfortunately, I do think that being constantly teased about my looks from a young age is at the root of most of the body image and appearance issues that I still sometimes struggle with today. If you hear "you're ugly" enough, you begin to believe it.

I have one brother whom I actually didn't meet until I was starting high school. He is the only sibling I have on my dad's side, and he lived back East with his mom. Even though we spent no time together during our childhoods, I have the most in common with him. Even now, I am closer to him than I am to any of my other siblings.

My brother Mark committed suicide when I was 8 years old. Other than family pets, this was my first experience with death. Obviously, this had a huge impact on the whole family, and I will write more about this in a later chapter.

My sister, Laura, passed away from an accidental overdose about 9 years ago. She and I shared a room until I was about 10. She was incredibly beautiful inside and out. She had beautiful brown hair, striking blue eyes, and a gorgeous smile. She had a big personality and the best, most infectious laugh in the whole world. When I was young, I really looked up to her; I wanted to *be* her.

My oldest brother has proven time and again that he is a master manipulator and out only for himself. He has no regard for others. For this reason, I choose not to have a relationship with him. This may sound harsh – after all "he's family". But we still get to decide who we surround ourselves with, and I do not want to be around that negativity at this point in my life.

I don't remember a whole lot about my childhood life with my siblings – not even with Laura, and we shared a room. I was significantly younger, and the age difference was enough for all of them to be off doing their own things while I was growing up. I do credit, my well-rounded love of music, to them, though. They all listened to different genres, so I was turned on to a lot of great music. My sister's playlist was definitely the biggest influence.

My parents separated when I was about 9, and divorced when I was in the 6th grade. My mom was left to raise 5 kids on her own, and that meant she was out of the house working a lot. I honestly don't remember her around much at all. When she *was* home, she was usually in her room with the door shut. She secluded herself to smoke pot, but I also think she was grieving my brother behind closed doors. Or maybe she was just detaching to avoid feeling anything at all.

The main form of communication between my mom and us kids, was notes. She would leave notes for us, and we would leave notes to her. This made for a very distant relationship between the two of us in those days. Later, in my adulthood, we became much closer. We had been best friends for about 18 years. She passed away about 7 years ago from health issues.

My dad and I keep in pretty close contact now, and I really value the relationship I have with him at this time in my life. Although I don't remember him being present in my childhood very much, I do have some fond memories.

The top 5 things I love most about myself are:

1. My witty sense of humor. I'm seriously funny. I crack myself up all the time!
2. My ability to see the good in any situation. I will almost always find the collateral beauty.
3. My willingness to learn. I never want to be the smartest person in the room. If I am, then I'm in the wrong room!
4. My deep desire to be the best version of myself possible for myself and for you.

5. Perhaps most importantly, my enormous capacity to love, despite all of the trauma I've been through.

⁓

I am a full-time professional nanny. I also do holistic healing work, when time allows. I love what I do for a living! I'm not getting financially rich from it, but I am able to support myself, and I have everything I need. I find my work very meaningful and fulfilling. This is wealth to me.

I am single and have been since my divorce about 8 years ago. I am a mom to three absolutely amazing human beings. They truly are the greatest things I have ever done, and I honestly believe this world is a better place because they are in it! I was able to stay home to raise them for a large part of their childhoods, building a very solid relationship with each of them; I connect deeply with each of my children on different levels, different genres, and in different aspects of life.

⁓

Amber is my oldest at 28. I turned 19 right after she was born, so we kind of grew up together. She is her own woman now, but we are also best friends. Of course, I am first and foremost her mom and am there for her in that capacity when she needs me to be. It brings me great joy that we have the kind of relationship where we can tell each other anything. We think very similarly for the most part; when one of us gets irrational, the other brings her back to reality.

My divorce was probably one of the hardest times in my life, and I was an absolute shitshow. At the age of 21, Amber was my rock. There was a bit of role-reversal at that time. Looking back, I know it was very hard on her, and I know it wasn't fair for me to lean on her so much. But I also think it helped bridge the deep friendship we have now.

Amber and I share deep conversations about very 'out of the box' subjects. We talk about metaphysical topics on occasion, and I believe she has mediumship abilities. We talk about connection with people in life, and in death. We talk about the afterlife.

Amber's dad passed away when she was a week shy of 16 – fallout from his life of drugs. Perhaps, as a result, Amber has an intense understanding of loss and grief and is extremely open-minded. She is an old soul, wise beyond her years!

Amber and her husband Ryan have given me two beautiful grand-babies, Camden David and Rowan Marie. Now, Amber and I talk about mom stuff too. I love that she looks to me for advice and guid-ance in that area. It tells me she likes who I am as a mom and that she likes herself. It tells me that she is comfortable with her childhood, and wouldn't mind raising her children with a similar parenting philosophy.

Dylan, 24, is my second child. Even now, he likes to play the "middle child" card when he doesn't get his way. He and I are alike in our excellent senses of humor! See what I did there?

From the day he was born, Dylan was a very free-spirited person. I was very much that way too, when I was little. I lost that free spirit as I grew up; maybe it was trauma, maybe it was just the cynicism of being an adult. As a child I was like sunlight! As an adult the darkness took over and I had a lot of fear. I felt I needed to appear perfect which came with it, an illusion of some sense of control. So, needless to say, free-spirit and control freak don't really mesh well together, so my free-spirit was stifled. But Dylan helped me rediscover this joyous part of myself during the period after my divorce.

Dylan and I went on what I like to call a "Soul Journey". We trav-eled through four states, Arizona, Colorado, Utah, and California.

We visited and stayed with some family and friends throughout the two-week adventure. One of our stops was visiting my cousin, who is a monk, at his Buddhist monastery in Northern California. It was incredibly beautiful there, both in nature and in spirit. The wisdom my cousin shared with us during an impromptu yet deep conversation helped both Dylan and me along our Soul Journeys. Seeing the peaceful, beautiful life that one could live, with only the most necessary possessions and seemingly endless time to meditate, was very enlightening. It actually felt magical to me. Dylan remembers that peek into the monastic lifestyle as one of the coolest experiences he's ever had.

My Soul Journey with Dylan was one of the most free-spirited things I had done since I was very young. I let go of my need to control and plan every detail; we just got in the car and went. We had so much fun! I think that was when I began to allow my own free spirit to re-emerge.

Dylan doesn't like to talk about otherworldly or spiritual stuff like his sister and brother do, but his connection with music is, I believe, otherworldly and very spiritual, even if he doesn't think so. He and I connect deeply through music. We both feel music from deep within; music helps each of us cope with life's struggles, and helps us heal. Our most recent outings together have been to reggae concerts. I like to joke with him and tell him that he must have been a Rastafarian in a past life. It might not be a joke, who knows?

Dylan doesn't really like to talk about his emotions either, but I believe that he feels like he can come to me with anything he has on his mind. It may not always feel comfortable for him, but I genuinely think he feels safe confiding in me. He has a huge heart and cares deeply about people, especially underdogs. Dylan and his wife, Blane, have given me two beautiful grandbabies, Deegan Blane and Bryce Celestine.

My youngest, Chandler, is 18. He just graduated high school this year. He also took second place as a senior, in the state of Arizona, at 195lbs in wrestling. I had to throw that in! That is a huge accomplishment that happens for very few.

We've always said Chandler is an old man in a young body. This guy has a wisdom that I have not really seen in any other 18-year-old. In fact, he has always seemed wiser than his peers, even when he was very young. You can ask anyone who has met him; I'm sure they would agree.

Chandler tends to be very biblical in his spiritual beliefs, yet he is still open-minded. I think I have had the deepest spiritual conversations of my life with him. We talk about Jesus, aliens, the stars, energy in crystals, Mother Nature, music (he plays guitar and is an avid music lover), and so much more. For a time, he was very big on biblical prophecies, and we talked a lot about what the second coming might look like. We also discussed the idea that there could be interpretations of bible verses that are very different than those that are generally accepted. I love Chandler's ability to talk about what is meaningful to him. I love his sense of life and awareness – that there truly is so much more to life than meets the eye.

I think Chandler came into this life with not only a lot of wisdom, but also a lot of karmic baggage – more than his fair share, for sure. Because of this, I think that it might be a big possibility that he has the potential to clear a lot of karma for multiple souls or lives. I truly think that if he can work his way through his own inner demons, it will in turn be a karmic clearing for many others.

Chandler's challenge has been that he is super hard on himself and can be very pessimistic. This seems to have been a part of his personality from day one – an innate characteristic. Of course, this can be painful for him. My hope is that, through my unrelenting positivity, I am being a way-shower and a light-bearer for him, ultimately easing his burden.

I was a single mom of two young children when I reunited with the man I would marry. We went to high school together and he is definitely one of the good guys. He stepped in and became the doting father my kids deserved.

We had, for the most part, a pretty great marriage. Well, maybe it was more of a partnership. We didn't fight much, and to the outside world, it seemed like the perfect marriage. And in some ways it was – it was very safe and comfortable.

But, something that I couldn't pinpoint was missing for me. Our marriage lacked passion and intimacy on so many levels. I had no idea at the time how extremely important that missing piece was for me. I carried on, playing the part of a happily married woman.

After 13 years of comfortable partnership, our separation and divorce came as a shock to pretty much everyone in our life, especially our kids. I think it was hardest on Dylan at the time, but about 5 years later, conversations with Chandler showed me it was pretty hard on him too. Amber was already out of the house so it didn't affect her in the aspect of not having her mother at home like it did the boys. It did affect her in how she ended up supporting me emotionally though.

I didn't leave my marriage because it was a bad marriage. Somehow, deep within myself, I was feeling a pull from the Universe. I knew there was a very important destiny waiting for me that would never come to pass if I stayed married. The pull I felt reached through my entire being. It was a deep, deep ache, a longing to fill a crucial and demanding void. I had cloistered myself in a safe place, away from the darkness, but I knew that there was a reason for all I had endured… a reason much bigger than myself. I had to explore it.

I was the one to move out because the property our home sat on belonged to my in-laws. Also, I was spending most of my time taking care of my mom, who was on in-home hospice care. It made more sense for me to move in with her, and for the boys to stay with my ex in what had been our family home.

I had been a stay-at-home mom up until the last year or two of our marriage. I went from being there 24/7 for the boys to not being there at all. Even though my mom lived only four houses up the road, this new situation was obviously quite a disruption for all of us. I wanted to keep home as intact as possible for the boys, so when I moved, I took very little: my personal items, a few childhood pieces of furniture, and some miscellaneous items. I even left all three of our dogs, who were my babies as well. I didn't want my boys to have their whole world torn apart, separated, and divided. I left it all.

⌐‿

Even though I was the one who wanted the divorce, that year was the darkest time of my life. By the time we separated, I had already been broadsided by the death of my sister, whom I had adored, and I had been taking care of my mom in hospice for several months and years prior to hospice. I think that was my second time around in my life experiences with the dark night of the soul. I wasn't considering suicide, but I also didn't care whether I lived anymore. I wasn't sure if there was a way out of this dark place.

⌐‿

When the divorce was finalized, I began that traditional journey of "finding myself", but it was much deeper than the cliché. Newly single, I of course felt very alone, but somehow, in this new reality, I came to believe that someone new was destined to enter my life. Together, we would do something big, something that would ripple love and healing into the world around us.

So, as far as I was concerned, my fate was set. I fully believed my divorce happened in pursuit of this far-reaching, healing destiny – a destiny that required a new partner. But, why hadn't I met this person? Why was I still single?

I purposely launched myself into a journey of self-discovery. I realized that I couldn't welcome whomever came into my life until I discovered who *I* really was. For seven years, I watched and waited. For seven years, I was on the lookout. Who would it be? Where could our journey take us? What impact would we make on the world?

I can't pinpoint the moment the realization hit me, but it was sometime during that seventh year, while I was entrenched in an intense program that would ultimately help me heal from my personal traumas. It was during this time that I finally came to understand that *I* was the person I was waiting for. As I painfully peeled back the layers of my experiences, I realized that the reason I left my marriage was not so that I could meet some new partner, but so that I could finally meet myself.

How can I express the impact of this epiphany? I – Audra – that freckle-faced, red-headed, pudgy eleven-year-old – was equipped with the power to heal. I was bursting with pain, love, and awareness, and I was willing to share it. This was a recipe that could help so many people. The device? A book. A book in which others could see their own traumatic experiences and find hope. Readers might realize they aren't alone, that the demons they are fighting have been defeated before. They can hope; they can heal.

I honestly believe that staying in that relationship would have meant my emotional and spiritual end. My traumas would have remained cloaked behind the masks that I thought society dictated I must wear. I would have continued to house an insurmountable amount of trauma, pain, and grief without ever even really knowing it existed. I would have suffered in silence, bleeding internally, until my death. With the traumas in control, I would never have found the will to launch my journey of self-discovery. I could not have had the strength to expose those experiences for others to see. The power I have now found – the power to provide hope, help, and healing for other trauma survivors – would never have revealed itself.

That marriage was, for the most part, a very comfortable place to hide. We don't tend to do uncomfortable things when we are comfortable. Self-discovery has been uncomfortable. Healing has been uncomfortable. Writing this book is uncomfortable. When people ask me why we got divorced, rather than blowing their minds with all this, I just say, "We loved each other enough to let each other go." To me, that is the beautiful truth of it.

⌒

About a year ago, I started counseling for past traumas that had never been worked through, processed, or even discussed, for that matter. As I mentioned earlier, I had a brother commit suicide when I was very young. When I was 14, my stepdad told me about his desire to molest me; when I was 17, he actually attempted to. Later that year, I was raped by a peer. When I was barely 20 and a new mom, an uncle attempted to murder me by trying to beat me and strangle me while I slept.

At the time, none of these events were addressed or worked through; some were not even acknowledged. My family coped with trauma by not coping with it. We did not talk about uncomfortable things. So, I was on my own. I was a good student, and I did what I was taught to do. And like a good member of my family, I just buried it all and said I was fine with a smile.

I was very good at burying each event. I was so good that it took a lot to get me through this healing journey; the events had been buried so deeply that I was unaware they were still affecting me.

Throughout my life, I have felt very alone as I carried these burdens. In an attempt to give myself a voice, the voice I never had, I shared much of my journey on social media. During counseling, I came to realize that there were many people out there who struggled the same way. So I realized that as I shared my journey, I was letting these survivors know they were not alone. As a result of my posts, many people told me that my journey was so compelling that I should pursue a broader platform; I have so much to offer the community of trauma survivors by sharing my story. I've repeatedly been told, "You need to write a book."

So, here I am! Indeed, some of the collateral beauty that has come from all my trauma is that I might have something helpful to offer! If I am able to help you, my own pain has more meaning. I will lead you in by sharing the stories of the last couple of catalysts that painfully led me to the realization that I had some serious healing work to do. From there, I'll share what the counseling process was like for me. Fair warning: I'd like you to walk with me through some of the sessions, some of the homework, and some VERY EXPLICIT details of the traumas.

You will see some of my Facebook posts that I posted as I was going through counseling, so you can catch a glimpse of what it looked like for me. You'll be able to see in real-time the awareness that was beginning to come forth, the fruits of my labor, so to speak. As well as showing you some other aspects of my life and myself, I will be sharing some of what I've learned and how I've grown. I am very humbled for you to take this journey with me. My hope is that somehow it touches you.

Through that touch, I wish you hope, light, love, and healing.

CHAPTER 3

THE HOUSE OF MIRRORS

The energy you give off based on your beliefs, your emotions,
your behavior, the vibrational frequency you give off, is what determines
the kind of reality experience you have because physical reality
doesn't exist except as a reflection of what you most strongly
believe is true for you.

That is all that physical reality is. It is literally like a mirror.

~Darryl Anka

bout three years after the divorce, I decided to get serious about dating, so I re-entered the dating pool. This
is supposed to be exciting and fun, but of course, it was
complicated. I kept having the same type of shitty experience and I
could not, for the life of me, understand why. I believe in energy and
the law of attraction. I see myself as a kind, loving, giving, and honest
person, so I should have been meeting that type of person. I genuinely
felt that the men I was meeting were quite the opposite. What I was
experiencing was not at all matching my energy. It took me a few really
painful experiences and a whole lot of self-reflection to finally look at
the common denominator: me!

While these experiences were painful at the time, they really turned out to be catalysts in bringing awareness to my wounds, ultimately catapulting me into the hero's journey.

⌐

"AFG"

I met this guy on a dating website. You may be saying to yourself right now, "Oh girl! You needn't say anything more!" But I had actually heard many success stories about online dating, so I thought I'd give it a try.

The man I met was attractive in his photos, but more importantly, I liked what he had to say about himself. He said he was divorced for 6 months, a father, a psychotherapist, and in the Air Force. Someone in that occupation sees, on a daily basis, what dishonesty and deceit can do to a person. Surely he wouldn't be out creating the damage that he was trying to facilitate in healing, right?

I was a little concerned that he had only been divorced for 6 months. It seemed like that wasn't enough time to get over a long-term relationship and join the dating scene. But someone in his line of work would know if he was ready.

I felt we had a lot in common, too. We were both divorced and single parents; we were both interested in helping others heal; and while I had been a Psychology major for the two years I attended college, he had finished his training in that field.

I'll call him Air Force guy, AFG for short. We talked for almost a month before we finally met. We talked on the phone, texted, and emailed several times daily. The topics and our discussions were much deeper than your typical surface conversations. We shared with each other what was genuinely meaningful to ourselves. Needless to say, with so much deep and intimate communication, on some level, I felt I had fallen for him before we ever even met.

When we did finally meet, it was like the fourth of July in my heart. I was already mentally and emotionally attracted to him, and now I was physically attracted to him as well. Things happened with us physically, very quickly. We kissed, held hands, hugged, and touched a lot the first time we met. We were fully intimate with each other the second time we met.

Looking back, he did give me all kinds of signs, warnings, and red flags, and subconsciously I chose to ignore them. I am sure it was because, like everyone, I just wanted to be loved or feel loved. In my mind, he was perfect for me. In reality, he was a player.

It turned out he was still married! Not just still married as in, separated, haven't-signed-the-papers yet, but actually living with his wife and child, no intention of divorce, still married! He said he was extremely unhappy in his marriage and that he was completely in love with me, but he was not willing to leave her. When this finally hit me, I was devastated to say the very least!

But wait, there's more. He was going to be re-stationed far away, and he was taking his wife and not me. His explanation was that he wanted his child in his life daily, so he was leaving me behind. I didn't blame him for choosing his child over me, and actually, I admired him for wanting to be a father to his child, but I felt like such a fool nonetheless!

I felt so deceived and ashamed. I was the Other Woman – the woman who falls in love with another woman's husband. I know I'm being hard on myself here. I acknowledge completely that he lied to me, so it wasn't really my fault at all, but the shame was there all the same. I can't even begin to put into words the shame and humiliation I felt.

When he left, I was beside myself with grief. In that grief, I busied myself and did some investigating. Yes, on top of everything else, I was now a stalker, too. I discovered more lies that he had told. He had even lied to me about his name. I had fallen for a man and had been emotionally and physically intimate with him, and I hadn't even been calling him by his real name. I felt so incredibly violated and betrayed! Angry is definitely not a strong enough word – I was furious with him – and with myself for having fallen for it!

You would think that once I found out he was married, I would have been angry enough to say goodbye. Certainly learning that he used a fake name with me – that would have done it. Or how many kids he really had, or the countless other lies would have been enough for me to say goodbye. But no. I decided to hang on to a long-distance, emotional relationship. Seriously, what was wrong with me? How had I become this person?

Even as I kept returning to him, I struggled tremendously with his lies. I tried to understand him, myself, and this relationship for almost four years. Let me say that again, "Four years!" Even though I didn't want to cause pain to another human being, I still wanted him to choose me. I wanted him to show me that I was worth the investment and that he couldn't live without me. I wanted him to show me that the power of love was real and that I was worth it. So I continued to invest in him.

It never happened; he didn't choose me. But I still couldn't work up the courage and self-worth to walk away from him. I told myself that maybe he wanted to choose me, but didn't have the courage to leave his unhappy marriage. Or that he wanted both a marriage and a loving relationship.

Somewhere in those years, through all the anger and disgust I felt towards him and myself, I managed to find some compassion and understanding. Through a lot of therapy, homework, and self-reflection, I found some forgiveness for myself and for him. During the relationship, I obviously didn't realize it, but I eventually came to understand that he wasn't much different than I was — we both were in a lot of inner pain. He wanted to feel loved, worthy, and chosen, just like I did. He was crying out for help through his actions and inappropriate behavior. He was allowing himself to be a part of unfulfilling relationships in a quest for acceptance, just like I was. He needed love for himself, just as I did.

I had entered the dating scene looking for a relationship with someone who would mirror my positivity. Instead, AFG and I mirrored each other's reckless quests for acceptance to one another. Seeing it clearly now, I see so much tragic beauty in it.

And it *was* tragic. We had connected deeply on so many levels: in conversation and how we undeniably experienced each other physically. It could have been so right. But it destroyed my trust.

My biggest struggle was that I questioned our true feelings and love for each other. He continued to tell me how much he loved me, but how could he love someone that much and not choose them? How could I really love someone who had told me so many lies? How could I love someone when I might not even really know him?

It turned everything into a lie for me. I couldn't tell truth from fiction anymore. I couldn't even trust my own personal, first-hand experience. I lost the ability to trust myself, my judgment, and my feelings... about everything. Worse, I didn't even know who I was anymore. I felt like a stranger to myself, and I blamed him.

I also struggled deeply with the possibility that he had not told his wife the truth about us, even though he said that he had. In my heart, I felt that she was just one more woman, alone in the world, incapable of making decisions about her life, her relationships, or her body based on the truth. Because there was no truth.

⌒

Towards the end of that four years, AFG turned out to be a major catalyst and a huge support in the next phase of my journey. My relationship with AFG was one of the more challenging experiences in my life. It was also some of the most painful lessons I have ever learned. However, I will be forever grateful for him and the entire experience. There is much, much more to this story and to AFG's contribution to my journey, which you'll read about in later chapters.

⌒

"PTG"

I also met this guy on a dating site. I know, I know, "Girl!!!" right? Again, on paper, this former police officer and current fitness trainer seemed like a stand-up guy, or at least a man of integrity.

Let's call him Physical Trainer Guy or PTG for short. We hit it off right away, but it was definitely just a physical attraction. I figured this out after a couple of dates. I saw it for what it was, basically a potential for friendship and a physical connection with another human.

We tried to make it work, on several occasions, as a traditional couple. We were unbelievably compatible sexually, but we just weren't compatible as people.

Part of our connection was built on his constant assurance that he really cared about me, and I really wanted to believe him. I know *I* cared about *him*. I truly didn't have a problem with a "friends with benefits" relationship, but I felt that he didn't really feel the "friend" part. I think he used his words to play the part, but in reality, he just said what he thought he had to say to keep the amazing sex coming. I was feeling used.

But again, I wanted to believe his words. I wanted to believe that he at least cared about me as a person and wasn't just straight up using me like a soulless piece of meat with no feelings. I wanted to believe him, because even though I didn't want a traditional relationship with him, I also didn't want to accept that I was allowing myself to open up my sacred body to a man that really didn't give two shits about me as a person. I didn't want to believe that I was that damaged, that I had such low self-worth and self-love that I would allow myself to be used like I was nothing.

I am aware that his actions and everything he lacked was a reflection of himself, his own wounds, and where he was in his own evolution. But as I am sitting here reflecting, I can't help but ask myself the question, "What did this man mirror to me?"

Although I now see PTG as a catalyst into my hero's journey, in layman's terms, PTG was a disgusting, lying, jerk. His inability to see the woman before him as a human being with a soul, his lack of integrity, the sorry way he treated me – all of this was a perfect reflection of how I had been treating myself and how I felt about myself. Although at the time I had no idea, it was a perfect reflection of my lack of self-love and self-worth. This is why my subconscious allowed this to happen. I had such a big heart when it came to others, but when it came to myself, I didn't count.

My self-esteem was shot. This two-year, on-again, off-again situation was happening during the same four year period as my relationship with AFG. I met PTG about six months after AFG had moved.

PTG and I discussed our situation on several occasions and decided to just be friends with benefits, basically. I don't know why I use the word "friends" – friends don't manipulate and use each other. But it does capture the idea that we were amicable, and we had sex.

I did make it very clear that I was not interested in being one of his "girls", so if he was seeing anyone else, he had to be honest about it. The thought of being one of someone's multiple, concurrent sex partners, sickened me, and I told him that. I made it very clear to him that it was very important to me, as I feel it would be to anyone, that I be able to make choices about opening my body to him based on the truth. This was a point I needed to drive home after my experience with AFG. I told PTG that I would extend the same courtesy to him.

But I would be betrayed.

One Fourth of July evening, we were at his place watching a movie. He received a phone call and then said that his aunt had been in a terrible car accident. He needed to get to the hospital right away, because they weren't sure if she was even going to make it. I of course left so he could attend to his family.

I remember this night vividly. I watched the fireworks in the skies all around me as I drove home. It was profound for me, witnessing something so beautiful while he might be witnessing the death of his aunt. I cried all the way home. I felt so sad for him and for his family. I prayed for him, his aunt, and their family for weeks until he finally told me she was in the all-clear.

We didn't talk much after that. About four months later, he reached out and told me he was moving for work. He wanted to see me before he left to say goodbye. I knew this was a clumsy code for one last bout of sex. I had decided months before that I was done being used, so I told him, "No!" He made a genuine effort into sweet-talking me into it, but I stood firm with my no. At least, now, I was standing up for myself in this relationship.

A few months later, I was checking out PTG's Facebook page, to see what he was up to and how he was doing. As I scrolled down his timeline, to the timeframe of our relationship, I noticed there were intimate comments from another woman. What a blow. I knew that PTG was not the guy for me in the long run, but I thought he would at least honor my one request.

I was done with cheating men. I was done with their lying. I was done with their manipulation. I was done with making choices about my body based on lies. I was done not knowing the truth about the man I was with while another woman was likely in the same predicament. I was just done!

So I reached out to her because I felt she had a right to know. We talked and traded information. I found out that his aunt was never in a car accident. It was a lie to get me out of his house because his angry girlfriend was on her way over. Meanwhile, he was lying to her to come and see me.

He made it all up. He was able to come up with a detailed lie, about his aunt on a moment's notice. He knew how upset I was for him and his family, and it was all a lie!

It should come as no surprise that his move was also a lie. The girlfriend and I figured that the "move" was at about the time the two of them were getting really serious and about ready to move in together. He decided to come to me after he had already been with her for months because he wanted to have sex with me, one last time before they moved in together. Seriously, how gross is that? What kind of man does that!?

She also told me there were multiple women she had found out about. This could very well mean that there were other women while he and I were together. Again, I felt violated. Again, I had not gotten to make choices about opening my body to someone based on the truth, despite having the conversations around it.

WHO WAS "DATING AUDRA"?

I had really begun looking at the past four or five years and began asking myself questions about my romantic relationships. Why did I keep having the same type of crappy experiences? It was like I kept falling in with the same man over and over again! Each was a different body, but in essence, they were all the same person.

From time to time, I had done some evaluating over the years, trying to understand it. But this time, I was digging much deeper. I was tired, deeply hurting, and didn't want to continue feeling the way I did. I felt an inner drive to figure out what was going on. What was it about Dating Audra that she kept getting involved in such negative relationships?

My internal barrage of questions went something like this: "Why am I not meeting a good guy when I am such a good person? Why do I keep meeting men that use me? Why do none of them want to truly invest in me, when all the other people in my life consistently tell me how amazing I am? Why do I keep meeting men that are so dishonest when I am so honest? Why am I putting up with it, when I know I deserve so much more? What is wrong with me?"

I felt so unlovable and could not find understanding around it. The law of attraction was clearly broken in my life! My experiences were not at all matching the person I thought I was.

I was in so much confusing, inner pain. When I looked at my reflection in the mirror, I saw a beautiful, long-haired, strawberry blonde woman with startling blue eyes and fair, freckled skin looking back at me. Look at her! She is so strong and courageous; she is gentle and kind. Her spirit was much too big for her body to contain. It radiated from within her.

But, when I looked deeper, I could see the sadness in her eyes. I could feel the despair in her soul. She was breaking her own heart by how she was allowing others to treat her. She was giving herself away to men who did not deserve her.

It took me a while to realize that, when I looked at her, I was missing the most important thing: I failed to see that part of that radiated strength and joy was the love she so freely gave to others. But she was not giving it to herself.

⁓

HEAL THYSELF

The healing world was where I found my center. Shortly after my divorce, I invested a lot of time in energy classes. I became a certified Reiki Master. I also got certified as a Master in Blue Star energy, as well as becoming a certified Karuna Reiki practitioner.

Shortly after my first Reiki class, my mom passed away. Along with a storm of pain and emotion, I was bluntly reminded of how brief our time is on this earth. So, at the age of 40, I quit the job I hated, as a banker, and I became a professional nanny. Here, I could freely give some of the love that was radiating from me to people who I knew would appreciate it: joyful, innocent children.

I put myself through school and got myself clinically certified as a hypnotherapist. I had hoped to start my own healing practice, but it was very challenging to get it off the ground. I loved doing the nanny work, and it was paying the bills, so I decided to do the hypnotherapy and energy work on the side, which is what I still do to this day.

But my struggles with dating was bringing me stress. With my college background in psychology and my education in energy work and hypnotherapy, how could I not figure this out? What the heck was I missing?

A few of my friends in the industry used to tell me that I needed to learn how to love myself first, before someone else could come into my life and love me. That used to just piss me off and send me over the edge! How dare they say I didn't love myself! Besides, it was obvious to me that some of these well-meaning friends weren't loving themselves either; of course, they couldn't see how much work I was putting in on my self-love. The nerve.

Look at how much I had accomplished: I left a comfortable life because I knew I was with the wrong partner. Isn't that self-love? I left a lucrative job that I hated because I knew I deserved a life I enjoyed. Isn't that self-love? So many people don't have the courage to do either one of those things to love themselves and I did both!

I saw people around me all the time that did not have self-love, yet they had intimate relationships! They were being loved and chosen! Why did they get to have someone loving them and I didn't? My friends would always remind me that not everything is as good as it seems from the outside... that those relationships were not the ultimate relationship that I was looking for. Logically, of course, I could agree, but it still felt cosmically unfair.

I was aware enough to recognize myself as the common denominator, but I genuinely did not know what the issue was. I was convinced that I knew myself pretty well: strong, kind, and loving... a woman deserving of a solid relationship. Of course, I knew that my father's absence during my childhood had resulted in some pretty deep-seated daddy issues and fear of abandonment. I felt that I had successfully addressed it on several occasions. I did a lot of work around that when I was in school for hypnotherapy, and I have had, for quite some time, a solid relationship with him that I truly value. At this time in my life, I had full awareness that my dad loved me and always had. I also knew that he had done the best he could with what he knew at the time, and that his departure was not a reflection of his feelings for me.

In short, I had been putting the work in to improve myself mentally, physically, emotionally, and spiritually. I had been putting the work in to be authentically Audra and to be my best self. For several years, I had been diligently working on me. So why was this happening to me? Not much later, I realized it wasn't happening *to* me, but actually happening *for* me.

CHAPTER 4

BREAKING POINT

Trust me, one night you'll be laying in bed looking over all your frustrations and you'll get tired. Tired of this same cycle, tired of settling, tired of hurting and tired of saying you're tired... and when that night comes that's when things will begin to change.

~Unknown

eliving the conversations with PTG's girlfriend left me angry all over again. I felt something inside of me snap. I was so disgusted! I was hurt, and I felt so violated again! I felt so ashamed of myself for being so stupid! I was so much smarter than this. Why did I allow this to keep happening to me? I did not deserve any of this! I felt I must have been a really REALLY bad person in a past life, because the experiences I was having with men since I was a little girl, did not match the person I am in this life.

Nine times out of ten, I am the optimistic, positive person. I see the light in even the darkest situations, the collateral beauty if you will. I also tend to see the best in people. This was one of the rare occasions where I saw nothing but darkness. I was done being emotionally pummeled by men. Having experienced a dad who left me feeling completely abandoned as a child, a dangerous stepfather who was intent on molesting me, a high school peer raping me, and an uncle attempting to murder me, I was finally hitting the wall.

These guys lying to me, to use me for my body, and to have their own selfish needs met, set all the dominoes in motion. This was the breaking point for me. I genuinely could not take anymore. I was done! I was done being the positive person! I was done seeing the brighter side of things! I was done seeing the goodness in people! I was done paying the price for other people's actions! Someone else needed to pay! Someone else, in all this mess, needed to be held accountable for their actions! I was tired of men getting away with this type of absolutely inappropriate behavior!

I found out quickly that PTG would not be held accountable. With everything his girlfriend already knew before I ever even talked to her, and even after she got a very clear picture from me of the lies and the actions this man was capable of, she stayed with him. Knowing that he was getting off scot-free made me feel like I had lost my sanity.

But I also had AFG from whom I could exact some justice.

I hadn't talked to AFG in probably six months. That was our pattern. In my emotional spin-out, I reached out to him and threatened to tell his wife the truth about everything. This was not the first time I'd threatened this either. It was however, the first time I was doing it solely out of pure spite.

The first time I threatened to out him to his wife was right after he left. I had found out that he lied to me about his name; I had, at that time, just gotten a full grasp of the reality of his situation and all the lies he had told. So I was going to tell his wife about my role in his life. It was a mess, a disaster. I think my wanting to come forward with the truth was a valid reaction from who I am as an honest person: the truth must see the light. I also legitimately felt that she had a right to know. At the time, though, I decided it was not my truth to tell.

The second time was about a year later. He had expressed to me how unhappy he still was in his relationship, despite having been in counseling with his wife for a year. I had a lot of mental anguish around all of it still. I still hadn't recovered or healed, at all, from any part of the situation with him.

He was so unhappy and said he loved me so much. He continued to tell me that he had never experienced love like that he had felt for me, nor would he ever experience it after me. He was miserable with her, and in love with me, and it still wasn't enough. The fact that he professed profound love for me, yet wouldn't leave an unhappy relationship, left me feeling like I wasn't enough, like I had no worth. I realize that it is complicated, and this is a very skewed way of seeing it, but it's exactly how I saw it and how I experienced it at the time. He told me that he had told his wife everything. But I was still deeply conflicted with the possibility that his wife did not know the truth of his feelings for me. I felt she had a right to make a decision about her life path based on the truth. Again though, it was not my truth to tell.

So now, after the disaster with PTG, here I was for round three of the threats to expose all. At this time, it had been three years since he left. At this point in my life, with all the reflecting I had done and realizations I had experienced, I knew there was something so much bigger and deeper happening within me. Yet, I didn't understand it at all. I didn't know how to deal with "it" because I still didn't know what "it" was. I didn't know how to help myself. But telling the truth felt like it could be cathartic, maybe even noble.

What was really happening was that I was screaming out for help with my own inappropriate behavior. I knew that I was using the threats as my own form of fear-based manipulation, to have my needs and wants met. It's humiliating to admit now that I was capable of doing the same thing that these men had done to me. I was capable of causing intentional pain due to my own selfishness. I was capable of manipulating to get what I wanted. I was hurting and wanted someone else to hurt too. The ripple effect, in full force, here folks.

AFG was able to talk me off the ledge, so to speak. At my core, I am not a mean or malicious person, and he knew that. Hurting someone else was not really what I wanted, despite the rage I felt. We both knew that. It was clearly a desperate cry for help and as a psychotherapist, he recognized that fairly quickly.

AFG and I started talking again frequently. He was to be restationed in about a month, and his wife and child had already moved, so he had a lot of freedom to be my emotional support. He began helping me unravel what was really going on with me, on a deeper level, just by listening to me. Something began to happen between us that had never happened: I started taking off the masks. I began getting honest with him and myself. I began to show him and myself the truth of the mess I really was. Are you seeing the irony here?

With AFG, I started talking about things that had happened to me, from which I genuinely thought I had healed. My upbringing taught me to sweep the unspeakables under the proverbial carpet, but they were still lurking there. For years, these men – this same man, over and over – kept appearing in my life to scratch the wounds I was never even aware I had. He kept showing up, opening wounds, and validating every horrible core belief I had about myself, although the beliefs were well-hidden from even myself. These beliefs had been created so long ago, buried so deeply within my subconscious, that there was no way my conscious mind could have realized they even existed.

These conversations with AFG served to lift the corner of that carpet. I had no idea of the ride I was about to go on as I lifted it to reveal my buried past.

It felt good to open up to AFG. Until these conversations, I felt like I had been suffocating, and now I could breathe again. For all of my adult life, I was sure I had been honest with myself, but I was clearly in some serious denial; I had been keeping my own secrets. I was unintentionally withholding information from myself, and therefore, from other people. Was I subconsciously using these men, with all their secrets and lies, to show myself the existence of my own? Is that why I sought them out?

Opening up to AFG was a very humbling experience, to say the least. Revealing all the trauma I had been through made me feel extremely vulnerable. But the vast chasm of fear that opened up beneath me was the realization of just how unhealed I was!

This revelation pushed me to look for my own counselor – someone who could really settle in for the long haul, and help me process and heal these wounds I now saw. Meanwhile, AFG and I continued to talk on a regular basis. Our conversations usually lasted for more than an hour; a lot of the time he would just listen to me cry.

As I heard myself narrating the traumas I had sustained in my earlier life, we both found a much better understanding of the real Audra, and why I had made the choices I did. AFG would later say that his love for me became stronger as he got to know the real, wounded me. I believed him, because my love for him grew as well: the ongoing intimacy we built that allowed me to open up to him, and the fact that he stayed – he didn't run for the hills – made my love for him stronger and deeper.

AFG was my counselor, before I started with my counselor. He continued to stand present and hold space for me as I brought more and more of my darkness into the light. He was also my friend. He was the first person with whom I was ever this real regarding my past. He was getting to know aspects of me at the same time I was. He stayed true, even though we were both discovering all the events that I thought made me unlovable.

One would think that these circumstances would offer the perfect foundation upon which to build a solid, life-long relationship. This level of trust and generosity is the very recipe for commitment.

But we didn't get there. He still had an emotional and obligatory role with his wife and child. We did discuss his situation sometimes, but it clearly made him feel very uncomfortable to do so. Maybe it was because he was still lying to himself about his own happiness. Once in a while, he would unveil some of his own relationship pain, but quickly paper it over again with a declaration of how well things were going at home. Somehow, I was able to unburden and discover myself, while he still felt the need to keep up his own facade.

Frequently, throughout my healing journey, AFG and I would acknowledge that we would one day need to leave each other behind. There would come a time when I would need to say goodbye to him for good. It seemed too difficult to imagine, but I knew it was true. As helpful as this relationship was for me, I knew that it was very dysfunctional; this was not what healthy love looked like. We both knew that I would get to a point where I didn't need him anymore, where the dysfunction would be too detrimental.

Whenever we talked about what this final separation might look like, the tears flowed for both of us. He was so gracious, and told me that it would be my decision. Until then, he was committed to standing present for me no matter what.

I realize that this segment of our relationship looks one-sided – that he was my vessel. Maybe it even looks like I was taking advantage of his generosity. But AFG made it clear he did not feel that way. He frequently told me how honored he was to share in this part of my journey. He appreciated that I was willing to trust him, even after all of his lies and the pain he had caused me. There was catharsis for him during this journey as well. He felt that he was working to redeem himself to me. At the very least, he was proving to me that his early declarations of love were never a lie.

As we neared the end of this leg of the journey, I was fully aware of the catalyst he had been. I tried to express the depth of my gratitude. If I hadn't been able to begin to unveil my deep secrets to AFG, I may never have realized why I was in the pain that I was in. Through our conversations, I was able to dip my big toe into the idea of counseling, and now I was ready to take the plunge.

CHAPTER 5

THE HERO'S JOURNEY

Her Time

She has been feeling it for awhile – that sense of awakening.
There is a gentle rage simmering inside her, and it is getting stronger
by the day. She will hold it close to her – she will nurture it
and let it grow. She won't let anyone take it away from her.
It is her rocket fuel and finally, she is going places.

She can feel it down to her very core – this is her time.

She will not only climb mountains – she will move them too.

~Lang Leav

*W*hat is the hero's journey?

Joseph Campbell (1904-1987), the American author and lecturer, realized that most epic myths are built on a structure he called "A Hero's Journey".

Through this journey, the hero was able to overcome whatever challenges were thrown his way, and in the process, the hero would develop into a much stronger version of himself. As a student of the human condition, Campbell also realized that we mere mortals might evaluate our lives through this lens, facing challenges and growing stronger.

In a very summarized version, the journey involves 12 stages set in a circular pattern. We see the hero's journey, time and again, in movies we watch, books we read, in the lives of others, and yes, even in our very own lives. Bob Riley famously said, "Hard times don't create heroes. It is during the hard times when the 'hero' within us is revealed."

And now, I invite you to join me on my very own, real-life, hero's journey! It begins with an overview, in the context of the 12 stages.

Stage 1: The Call to Adventure: The hero receives an invitation or a challenge. For me this was my Call to heal, my Call to look within myself and see what really resided there in the darkness. Only in this way would I be able to change the way I viewed and experienced life.

Stage 2: Assistance: Every hero needs a little help – a team that comes together to help them through their journey. My Assistance included the people (even the unpleasant ones) who acted as catalysts in my life, my friends, family, and my counselor.

Stage 3: Departure: The hero has accepted the call and crosses the threshold between what she has known and the unfamiliar. My Departure was walking into the counselor's office, willing to accept the outcome, without any understanding of how my life could forever change.

Stage 4: Trials: The hero begins to overcome obstacles, metaphorically slaying their monsters. This is when the heroic attributes that we all have within us begin to emerge. Even though the monsters are frightening, the hero is required to face them. My Trials were my encounters with my past traumas. I had to be willing to walk through the darkest hours of my past with a searchlight, with my eyes wide open.

Stage 5: Approach: The hero must face her biggest fears. She is beginning to really gain momentum! Approaching my traumas meant actually walking through and talking about them. It required that I fully acknowledge everything that had happened to me. It was allowing myself to feel whatever came with that acknowledgment, including the fear that still lived within me.

Stage 6: Crisis: This is the hero's darkest hour. It is at this point when we are not sure if the hero will emerge victorious, or be annihilated by the monsters. Metaphorically, it is a possible death of the hero allowing her to reemerge like a phoenix. At the end of this stage, if the hero survives, she is fully manifested! My Crisis came when I was finally able to realize how much my traumas had distorted my self-image. This is when I realized that I had been carrying manufactured beliefs for almost my entire life. It was the recognition that I had been experiencing my life based on these beliefs. I had to challenge all of my core beliefs, threatening a psychological self-annihilation, in order to realize how much my past had been affecting my present. It was a foundational crisis from which I was not sure I would be able to emerge. But when I did, it was glorious.

Stage 7: The Treasure: The hero claims the reward! She has saved the day! My Treasure was finally gaining full awareness of what had been taking place in my subconscious mind. I was able to set myself free and see, very clearly, what I once was completely blind to.

Stage 8: The Result: The hero makes it through the journey. Although the journey will always be a part of the hero, the monsters are defeated, at least for now. My Result was the completion of my, coincidentally, 12 weeks of therapy. It was the metaphorical transformation of the caterpillar into a butterfly.

Stage 9: The Return: This is nearing the end of the circle of stages when the hero goes back to her normal life. My Return allowed me to look back and reflect upon what I had just experienced and everything I had gone through up to this point in the journey.

Stage 10: New Life: The hero recognizes that she has changed and outgrown the old life that she left behind when she began the journey. My New Life included a new-found awareness in every aspect of my life. Everything was so much clearer, and I recognized that I had changed tremendously.

My life would never be the same.

Stage 11: Resolution: All the reasons the journey took place are resolved. All the loose ends are tied up. My Resolution allowed me to experience life completely differently. Everything I learned on my journey helped me to reframe my subconscious, and I was able to heal.

Stage 12: Status Quo: The hero has gone full circle, back to a regular existence, but one that is more befitting her hero status. My Status Quo means that I have integrated my new awareness and my reframed subconscious into an upgraded daily existence.

———

Joseph Campbell, through years of study, identified the Hero's Journey as one that occurred in most great myths; novelists and screenwriters use the same template in their work. I think the reason why we can be totally enthralled by a movie, a book, or a story is because we are really witnessing our *own* lives, playing themselves out in a slightly different form.

One could argue that the ultimate hero's journey is our life in its entirety. Can you see scenes from your own life resembling this journey? Can you see yourself as the hero? If your answer is no, I encourage you to look a little harder; your hero is there.

———

My journey really began when I realized that I no longer wanted to live the fear-based life I was living. I no longer wanted to be triggered negatively by the people around me. I wanted to heal and take the steps necessary to become my best self. This was my challenge, and I accepted. Now, let's take a look at this journey in its entirety.

Audra Weeks
September 23, 2017 ·

My open letter to the Universe.
To the ever so patient mirrors in my life, past, present and future. Thank you for seeing and feeling my innate beauty and reflecting it back to me.
To those that choose me, past, present and future. Thank you for seeing, feeling and knowing my inherent worth.
To those standing present, past, and future. Thank you for seeing, feeling and knowing that I need you.
Thank you to myself for having the courage to take this healing journey and
For not being afraid or ashamed to share it!
PEACE and LOVE

 31   14 Comments

"I genuinely want to be my best self in every aspect, for myself and for others. I know what I want to experience, and I am working on not settling for less. I will not stifle myself to feel comfortable in a situation, or to fit, or be what others need or want me to be.

I am completely willing to shatter myself, and be shattered in order to be released from the old story that's full of lies, so that I can step into and live the truth of who I know I truly am, and what I truly deserve to experience.

I am a loving, caring, passionate, beautiful woman who is capable of expressing herself on so many levels, and I can live and will live a life that has depth and deep intimacy on every level.

I make mistakes and that is ok, because it show the beauty of being human, and the vulnerability of being Audra. I deserve, and will have people and experiences come into my life that compliment and mirror back the goodness, passion, and beauty that is within me. I deserve to love in every facet. I am incredibly loveable, and so worth loving, so worth choosing, and so worth standing present for.

I am worth investing in, and I am paving the way, by investing in in myself, holding space for myself, choosing myself, and loving myself through all of this beautiful, and oh so uncomfortable pain. I am willing to do whatever it takes, and I am willing to give myself whatever I need.

I choose me."

CHAPTER 6

THE HEALING WORK

PART 1

*Soul work is not a high road. It's a deep fall into an
unforgiving darkness that won't let you go until you
find the song that sings you home.*

~Unknown

 Audra Weeks   • • •
August 30, 2017 • 👥

I start counseling tomorrow. I am embarking on a healing journey and major release regarding some past traumas.
This is exactly how I feel. I laugh because it's so profoundly funny and accurate.
I am so tired. Tired of carrying all this by myself. I'm tired of seeing how it's all affecting my life. The ridiculous, and very sad heartbreaking beliefs I have about myself that I adopted because of shitty things that I had absolutely no control over.
I would have addressed all this much sooner had I realized. I thought I was good. I'm not sure how I came to that conclusion, and how I held on to it for so long, through so many traumas, but it's genuinely what I thought.
Tomorrow is the day. The day I start burning this mother***er to the ground!
PEACE and LOVE

 90   59 Comments

"What day is today?" asked Pooh

"It's the day we burn this motherfucker
to the ground." squeaked Piglet

"My favorite day." said Pooh

THE INTAKE

*T*he day of my first counseling session had finally arrived! I had a plethora of different feelings that morning. I was so excited with a mix of some anxiety. I didn't really know what I was about to walk into, and that unknown gets us every time, you know? I don't think I really felt scared, it was more nervousness. I had facilitated so many healing sessions for my clients already that I felt there was really nothing new under the sun for me. I also had been to counseling for a few sessions when I was 20, shortly after my uncle tried to murder me, so it wasn't, in essence, my very first time with a psychotherapist. I felt somewhat experienced going into this.

It was very important to me that I meshed well with my counselor, so I had a bit of anxiety around that. I think I have a unique way of seeing and experiencing things. My thoughts and beliefs extend well beyond the perimeters of the traditional 'box'. It was crucial for me to feel that I was not being critiqued for who I am and how I see things. Would this counselor judge me for my unusual self-reflections? I needed to feel safe enough to be myself.

In the past, I had been very good at masking my true feelings, even with those closest to me. I felt safer that way. So it was challenging for me not to put on that mask as I walked into that office for the first time. But I knew that, in order for this to actually work, I had to be authentic no matter what I looked like to this stranger. I needed to fully trust the process. Showing up as my naked self was terrifying, but invigorating.

My counselor's name is Mireya. The first session was an intake session. She asked me a bunch of questions to find out what was going on and to get a feel for where I was at with it all. While she was internalizing me, I was internalizing her. We briefly discussed the traumas I was dealing with and my options of treatment. I realized that I had been suffering in silence for pretty much my entire life, so I felt it was crucial for me to have the chance to have a voice and the opportunity to voice and share my stories, out loud. I needed to speak them out, so I could actually process through and release the things that had happened to me from my body and my mind.

⌣

THE GAME PLAN

I decided to go with cognitive therapy, which would allow me to process how I was dealing with "the now" in the context of the trauma I had endured. It would help me understand how the trauma from the past was impacting my present.

It was only once I started therapy that I realized how alone I had felt for most of my life. My family's coping mechanism of "papering over" even shared trauma trained me to accept that no one talks about darkness, and that it must be borne alone. The silence throughout those decades was deafening.

I tend to feel and experience things on a pretty deep level. I see the irony and the humor in life, but I really experience things in a metaphorical sense, drawing parallels on multiple levels. It is clear to me that life, with its twists and turns through darkness and light, is a mirror of our inner worlds.

Expressing this part of myself and how intensely I am experiencing things can be very challenging. How does one explain the glory of a sunset to someone who has not experienced colors? What words could one use to describe the intensity of a habeñero pepper to someone who has tasted nothing spicier than vanilla? It has left me feeling very alone to be unable to effectively share the depth and intensity of my experiences, or when I feel that attempting it will leave me open to ridicule.

Certainly, the fear of being misunderstood has deepened my feelings of isolation. Cognitive therapy felt like a space where, even if my attempts at expression were ultimately unsuccessful, I could still explore without fear of judgment.

Mireya warned that the 12-week cognitive therapy program would be intense, and it would require me to do a lot of homework. I was excited and up for the challenge to heal, learn, grow, and change. I had absolutely no idea what I was in for. There was no fear in moving forward in this journey for me though. The only fear I had was, remaining where I had been, repeating those patterns that brought with them so much pain and confusion.

THE SUPPORT SYSTEM

Even with everything I've been through, I consider myself very fortunate to have quite a few dependables in my life. You know, the friends that you can always reach out to that will be there for you? I spread out what I was going through amongst them, giving each of them bits and pieces, but not the full picture. I had learned so well to pretend everything was okay even if it wasn't. I'm pretty sure that people's outside impression of me is that I have it all together. So I was so scared to let any of them know all of it. I was terrified to let anyone see how messy the inside of me really was. My entire life, people have looked to me for advice, inspiration, and strength. I didn't think my outside world could stand present for the hot mess that I really was. I know how strong I am, and I could barely handle it myself; how could I expect them to?

Besides AFG and my counselor, there were three friends in particular who knew more than anyone else: Lisa, who was my boss at the time, and my friends Leana and Jamie.

It was hard for Lisa not to find out; some days I would show up for work and I would have absolutely no control over my tears. Sharing this with my boss was of course very uncomfortable and embarrassing, but I knew I had no choice but to surrender to it. I had to allow it all to come; it was unstoppable. I would just have to deal with the fallout, however, that looked. It was terrifying to be so vulnerable with my employer, but I trusted her. And I was rewarded; I am so grateful for the friendship that evolved through that state of vulnerability.

Leana is actually one of my daughter's friends. She and I became very close friends when I started working with her, doing energy work, and doing some private classes. I was teaching her about chakras and meditation when she was going through a difficult growing period in her life. She was my daily support system. She helped me survive between my sessions with Mireya. Leana knew pretty much everything I was going through as I was going through it. She was also the only person, besides Mireya, with whom I was honest about my ongoing communication with AFG.

I have known Jamie since I was 18. We have been through a whole lot together. We were very close before I got divorced, and she has been my steady ever since. That woman has been standing present for me and all my mess the last seven years and continues to do so. We send a snap chat video to each other every morning and have for probably the last two years. I do not know if I would have made it sanely through the last seven years without her. She is a rock in my life.

These three held space for me and supported me no matter what. They witnessed a lot of tears, and had front row tickets to see my transformation. There truly are no words to express the gratitude I have for them, because I honestly do not know if I would have survived that 12 weeks without them! This is no exaggeration. There were times when it was more than I thought I could bear.

THE JOURNEY BEGINS

I was excited to talk to AFG about my first session and go over with him what Mireya and I had decided would be my best option of treatment. He agreed that cognitive was a good choice. I think I remember him chuckling when I told him I was excited about the homework. As a psychotherapist, he knew I had no idea what I was in for! He gave me a glimpse of what it might look like, but he was really good about not giving me too much information. I'm sure he knew it was important to my journey for it to unfold naturally without him leading the witness.

I had decided that I would be sharing my 'healing journey' on Facebook for a few different reasons. 1. I wanted to show people that they are not alone in whatever they are going through. 2. I wanted to show people that they can show up exactly as they are and people will still love them. 3. I wanted to have a voice and to let people see the real me. I was ready to take off the masks in front of my world. Looking back, I think I made sharing my journey look easy, but it wasn't. A lot of times, I would cry, ugly cries, after I posted, terrified of what my family and friends would think or just judgment in general. It felt so uncomfortable to be so outwardly vulnerable.

I was going to counseling once a week, so it was going to be one assignment each week. My first assignment was to show up at week two with impact statements about my traumas. Just a paragraph or so about each event to get the ball rolling, so to speak. I seemed to easily breeze through that first assignment. I was so excited about getting things rolling and to catch a glimpse of what the weeks ahead would look like.

I remember talking to Mireya about having a fear that things wouldn't change in my life. What if I do all this work and nothing changes? Logically I knew that was impossible because nothing ever remains the same, but I was still scared. That fear of the unknown again. My heart gently told me that it was going to be okay and to just trust the process.

My second assignment, heading into week three, was to write, in as much detail as possible, each trauma. I had five I was working through, so it was a lot to get through in one week. It left me feeling mentally and emotionally exhausted daily. I remember crying a lot that week. I had so much buried information coming forth that it was actually a mental overload. As a result, I was very forgetful in my daily routine. I never realized how much I had counted on that sense of control with my daily routine. I wasn't very present in the moment, either. It felt like I was walking around dazed and confused. I was in emotional survival mode, working through the actual realizations of everything that had happened to me. I didn't know how I was even still existing. Everything I had been though, all these traumas, just seemed like too much for one person to have to experience and survive.

Other than sharing some details on Facebook, I was isolating myself. I felt like I needed to close off the outside world to protect myself. I felt so uncomfortable and vulnerable. It was, and still is, very hard for me to trust people with my reality and my feelings. I am terrified that they are going to see me as weak, and that they will try to take advantage of my weakness to hurt me, use me, take advantage of me, judge me, abandon me... the list goes on.

My kids knew I was going to counseling, but we didn't really talk about it. They were as supportive as they could be without knowing everything that had happened, and that was happening.

It had to have been difficult for them and a hard dynamic for them to be in. To see their super-strong mom falling apart and coming undone, constantly standing in a pool of tears and vulnerability. I think maybe it made them feel powerless, because there was nothing they could really do to help me. It was surely hard for them to see this side of their mom. If they only knew how hard it was for me to let them see it.

Things started getting real for me in assignment two. Not only had that proverbial rug finally been lifted, but the dirt and dust was being beaten out of it. It was frightening to be so exposed to the truth and my emotions around it all. Good grief, my whole inner house was about to get a deep cleaning. The blinds were being drawn, and all the doors and windows were being opened up to this dark, hidden, inner world. I was starting to get my bearings within it, and began getting insight to what had been residing in that darkness for so many years.

CHAPTER 7

THE MISSING LINK

We didn't understand as children that our parents still
had work to do on themselves.

~Maryam Hasnaa

I promised myself that I would be honest and authentic to the best of my ability when I committed to writing this book. What I describe in these pages is truly the basis for so much of the pain in my personal life. This chapter was very challenging for me to write. I procrastinated by milling around in other chapters for hours that turned into days that finally turned into weeks of avoidance.

This chapter is challenging for me because I love my dad very much. I value the relationship we have now, and I have so much gratitude for his presence in my life. I know this chapter holds the possibility of causing him pain, and that is something that I am struggling with tremendously. However, I am also hopeful that this chapter will also allow us to understand each other better and deepen our relationship.

But I am not alone. I genuinely feel this chapter is going to hit home for many women. I know so many women, especially my age and older, who struggle tremendously with "daddy issues". Of course, some younger women have this struggle too, but as a society, it seems to have gotten so much better, which is huge progress!

It is only in the most recent generation or two that men have taken accountability for the most important aspects of parenting. Previously, the societal norm was that financial assistance was all that was required of a man, and in many cases, they didn't even provide that. I'm not condemning these fathers in any way. I know this is what society taught them and what society tolerated. Until men and women started really raising the bar of what being a father entailed, for their own well-being and that of their children, this was the norm. Unfortunately, this old norm created huge obstacles for generations of daughters to overcome in their adult relationships with men.

A girl's relationship with her father or father figure is the first experience she has with the opposite sex. This first relationship is, more often than not, going to pave the way for all of this little girl's future relationships. It is the template for all of her relationships with men. Society now accepts that a father's presence requires him to be a part of the day-to-day in the life of the child – spending quality time and expressing love through words, actions, and affection. If the father or father figure is not truly present, this child is going to have a whole lot of room to create stories about his absence. She might believe that she is not worthy of loving attention from a man, and accept this absence as the norm. The result is often a poor self-image that leads to toxic relationships. This was the case for me; my dad was not present. He did not show up for me when I needed him.

I think it's important to mention that to a developing child, there is a big difference between never having a dad in your life, and having a dad who chooses to be frequently absent. In either case, if that child is lucky, another trusted adult – her step-father or her mom's partner, for example – will come in and give the child what she needs to build a solid emotional foundation. But if her dad has *chosen* to be absent, the child will usually attribute his absence to her own lack of value. As a young adult building relationships, her diminished sense of value will fulfill itself. Her relationship choices will largely hinge on seeking approval while excusing the behavior of men who take advantage of her.

She will often choose men that will not show up for her in some aspect. That absence then reinforces her beliefs about how men should treat her. In a vicious cycle, her core beliefs about her own low value are constantly validated. This continues until (and if) she figures this out. She must then do the work to unravel these beliefs and replace them, finally realizing her own worth. This by itself can be a lifetime of struggle.

I really don't have any memories before 6 or 7 years of age. I am relying on the little I can remember along with the memory of others, including my dad, during that time.

I don't know how much he was around for me physically, mentally, and emotionally in those critical years from birth to age seven, or even until my parents got divorced when I was about 11. In fact, I don't remember whether he was a presence while he still lived with us. I can say that from the point of view of an angsty pre-adolescent, he definitely was not around enough. My core beliefs had already taken root.

Some might call my father a saint: When my parents were married, my mom already had five kids of her own under the age of 10. Let me say that again, *five kids*! My dad also had a son of his own who lived back in Illinois with his mom. An instant family of that size – less than 10 years of age – would have been a tremendous undertaking for any person. So, props to my dad for stepping in.

⌒

My dad worked construction. His work took him all over the valley and sometimes out of town. If his jobs were further away, that meant he would leave the house early and get home late. That didn't leave much time, if any, for him to spend with me, not to mention he had a wife and five other children who wanted his attention. If he was working out of town, he was generally gone all week and would come home on the weekends. He worked on really big projects, so he would be running a schedule like this for weeks or even months at a time.

It had to have been difficult for him. I know that he did make an effort in the early days and was trying to do what dads are supposed to do. He coached or assisted in sports with the older kids. I was still very little, so what was he supposed to do with me? After working and doing the dad thing with the older kids, there was very little quality time with me. He was doing the best he could and only had two hands and very limited time. Of course, as a small child, I had no understanding of this. I didn't really begin to feel that I wasn't getting what I needed from him until I was about eight or nine. He surely didn't even know, so how could I? Even though I wasn't aware of what the lack of a real father-daughter relationship was doing to me, the damage was being done. I wasn't receiving what I needed from him to grow into a healthy-minded teenager and woman; my subconscious was filing it all away.

About five years into the marriage, when I was about three, I think my dad was struggling in the father role. He may have been feeling that he had bitten off more than he could chew, marrying into five kids, having me, and his son in Illinois. Discussing this with him recently, he admitted that he had been completely overwhelmed in this role. My older brothers were becoming unruly in their teenage years, which added to the pressure and created a lot of stress in the house.

⌒

I participated in a variety of different activities growing up. I was in ballet and gymnastics; I also played softball and soccer. When my dad attended any of my events, it was a really big deal to me. It didn't happen very often. The worst were the broken promises – the no-shows – which crushed me. How could a child *not* internalize that? I wasn't a priority in his life. The absences and the broken promises fed my subconscious belief: my own father saw little value in me.

When my brother Mark got into his accident and later committed suicide, our house was never the same. Around this time, my dad began spending a lot of time at bars after work. He just seemed to disappear within my memories, as though he didn't even live with us. A year or two after Mark died, my parents separated, and my dad took a job in Tucson, about 90 minutes away. Because they were separated, he didn't come home on the weekends. I can count on one hand the number of times I saw him over the following two years. I can probably count on two hands the amount of times I even talked to him on the phone.

I was eleven years old, with all of the anxiety and drama of any pre-teen. On top of that, my brother had died, and my home was in emotional turmoil. My father's response was to move away. I absolutely felt completely abandoned by him. I felt that he did not care about me, and believed, for years, that he did not love me. Of course, now I know that he was going through his own issues, but at the time, how could I not feel this way? He did nothing to show me he cared. He made very little attempt to know who I was or what my life looked like while he was absent. From my perspective, he left and never looked back.

⌒

After my dad moved, he often forgot my birthday; on my most special day of the year, I wasn't worth remembering. He never made time for the two of us to spend together or even to talk. Everything else that requested his time was more important than I was. There was a lot of arguing between my parents about child support – my support. He seemed bitter about having to send money for my care; I was not worth his financial investment. During the separation and divorce, I felt that my dad resented me, that I was a burden, an unwanted financial obligation.

As I got older and started liking boys, I had a lot of insecurities. I had been picked on so much about my red hair and freckles when I was younger, even by those closest to me. I also had a lot of insecurities around not being enough or of value. When I started dating, my core beliefs drove my choices. Subconsciously, I was not worth much of a personal investment, yet I sought approval. So I chose boys who would validate those beliefs. These beliefs steered me away from the boys who genuinely saw me and adored me; they didn't fit with my internal idea of how a man should treat me. Instead, I gravitated toward boys who ignored or even belittled me, because this validated my view of a relationship. It's very sad, but this is what we do as humans when there are negative core beliefs on the subconscious level.

It took me decades to realize I had these internal beliefs. Once I saw them, I realized I needed to change them. I have been working on undoing them for years. It's a process that I'm still working through.

There's another facet to growing up with an absent father. Not only do you build warped ideas of relationships, but a father who has never been there for you cannot be a supportive resource for you later in life. As I got older and started going through some scary circumstances, it never occurred to me to reach out to my dad for help, and he never offered. He never offered me a place to stay when my stepfather began verbalizing his desire to molest me. I never asked my dad for anything that I can remember. I was too terrified he would say no; at age 14, the fear of being abandoned by him again was greater than the fear of facing my abusive stepfather. It was easier not to ask.

The point of this chapter is not to villainize my dad. In my heart, I know that if my dad had realized what his absence was doing to me, he would have done better. If he could have seen that I would grow up to believe I was not worthy of a healthy relationship and love, he would have made time for me. If he thought for a minute that my adolescent and adulthood would be littered with obstacles as a result of some pretty severe abandonment issues, he would have done things differently. There was no way for him to know.

The point of this chapter is to offer insight. Like many women, my earliest relationship with a man served to make it impossible to have a happy relationship later in life. Hopefully, some of these women will see themselves in my story. Maybe this will shed some light on their pain and offer them a starting point to begin to heal.

CHAPTER 8

MARK

*We talk about them, not because we're stuck or because we haven't
moved on, but we talk about them because we are theirs, and they are
ours, and no passage of time will ever change that.*

~Unknown

My brother Mark was an outgoing young man with a
bright future. Like many young men, he was still finding his path, but the possibilities were endless. By all
accounts, he was friendly and intelligent. He was a talented artist with
a great sense of humor.

When I was 7, Mark was in a horrific accident. He was only 17 at
the time. I don't remember a lot of the details but I'd like to tell you
what I have been able to piece together. Mark is no longer here in a
way where he can tell his own story. He can't share with the world who
he was or what happened to him or what he went through. To me,
he's so worth knowing! I would like for you to meet him, as much as
I can offer to you about him, even if it's only through the eyes of that
7-year-old little girl.

That afternoon, my parents came home with a bag full of bloody
and ripped clothing, a single beat-up shoe, and a cracked helmet.

Mark had been in a life-altering motorcycle accident. He had been making a turn, and the driver of the car did not see him. Mark was hit, and the motorcycle went under the car. I'm not quite sure where Mark ended up after the impact, but he was taken to the hospital, lucky to be alive.

There was a lot of discussion around the helmet, because Mark sustained a severe brain injury. He was in a coma for weeks. I desperately wanted to see him but back in that day, if you were younger than 12, you couldn't visit anyone in the hospital.

Even at seven years old, I could feel the tension and worry simmering in the house. My young age must have made me invisible while any discussions about Mark were taking place. I was certainly never invited to be a part of these discussions. I relied on eavesdropping in any conversation I could for my information. I can't imagine, at the tender age of seven, what thoughts, fabricated stories, and distortions of the facts that were swimming through my head. A bag of bloody clothes, sugar-coated details fed to me by the adults, the overheard whisperings amidst my siblings, and a seven-year-old's imagination gave me all manner of terrifying thoughts. As a nanny for a seven-year-old right now, I see the mental and emotional level. From that perspective, it is clear that a young child is not equipped to deal with such an event alone.

During Mark's recovery, my parents were M.I.A often, between work and trips to the hospital. Whether they were home or not, there was a lot of stress in the house. I may not have understood it, but I could definitely feel it.

It seemed like Mark was in a coma forever to me. (Relying on the memory of a family member, it was two or three weeks.) When he finally came out of it, another forever passed before he was moved to a rehab facility. Another forever later, he got to come home.

At least I got to visit him in the rehab facility. I only remember going once though. It was the first time I was actually going to get to see him, with my own eyes, after his accident. I was so excited! I was, however, briefed before we went. He was very different than I remembered him, so I was being prepped for the changes. I got the talk on rehab hospital etiquette. I had a pretty bubbly happy-go-lucky personality, and I was told, in no uncertain terms, to dial that down. I needed to keep it down because people were trying to rest and heal. I feel like what they should have added to that was, "Not too much happiness, Audra. People are busy being sad and depressed about their circumstances." Looking back and knowing what I know now, it probably would have been best to just let me go in there and be myself. Surely everyone there could have benefited from my bubbly happiness, loving heart, and joyful spirit – the best medicine for healing, in my opinion.

My brother was indeed very different. Before the accident, he was free-spirited and strong-willed. Mark had a lot of friends! I feel like everyone must have known him or at least had heard of him because of his wild side. He used to get himself into trouble A LOT! He and my oldest brother were partiers. It was the 70's; they listened to rock-and-roll, smoked pot, and were into some pretty hard-core drugs on occasion as well. He seemed to be very charismatic and happy. I remembered him being high-energy and dare devilish too! A thrill-seeker, if you will. Once, he had jumped off the roof of our house, just for the heck of it. He did stuff like that all the time! That's just who he was.

He seemed fearless to me. He was also an amazing artist! He could draw anything, but he was especially good at human faces. These were incredibly realistic portraits, and even more amazing given that he was just a teenager.

When Mark came out of the coma he was partially paralyzed on one side of his body. He was now blind in that eye also. I was so excited to be there, to see him and finally see what the heck was going on, but he just seemed irritated. I was little and obviously could not imagine what he was going through. He may have even been embarrassed. He definitely was not as excited to see me as I was to see him. The visit didn't last too long and I was grateful for that. It was very uncomfortable. I don't think I went back until it was time to bring him home.

Mark came home in a wheelchair. Because of the brain damage, and being partially paralyzed on one side, he had to relearn how to walk. He had to learn how to form words and speak all over again also. He did eventually learn how to walk again with the help of a cane, but that came slowly. He was still blind in one eye, but he was able to pretty much rehabilitate everything else. He even learned to do some really cool tricks in the wheelchair! The daredevil thrill-seeker was still alive and well. He would tilt back and ride on the back two wheels – wheelies! He seemed to do the best he could with the situation. He still tried to make light of things and have fun. I mean, he was still Mark despite how much was different.

But Mark had changed. He was still trying to recover brain function. He couldn't do the things he used to do, the way he used to do them. He didn't think the way he used to. At times, he even seemed child-like. He wasn't experiencing life the same at all. His artistic abilities left him; after the accident, he couldn't draw a face anymore. Without sight in one eye, he didn't have the depth perception to accurately proportion both sides of a face together.

When Mark first came home, his friends would come around, but as time went on, those visits became less and less frequent. He didn't really fit in with his friends anymore. I think his disabilities were more than his teenaged, partier friends wanted to deal with. My dad later told me that Mark told him, "they latered" him – they said "later" and didn't come back. My heart breaks at the thought. He must have felt so abandoned.

⌒

During his recovery and the emotional stress, there were a lot of angry outbursts from him. He would yell and throw things; he could be very destructive and scary to be around when he was mad. I'm going to make an assumption and say his fits of rage were out of frustration. He was frustrated on so many levels, about so many things. I can't even begin to imagine what he must have been going through.

He would tear out faces in magazines and use the magazine picture on the half he couldn't draw and then draw the other side to match. He said that this was how he felt – like half of him was real and alive, and the other half was fake and dead.

I'm not sure exactly how much time had passed since the accident – for how long Mark struggled with losing friends, losing abilities, losing his *essence*. I know he was 19 and I was 8 when he did it.

It was very deliberate – chillingly so. Mark found the key to my dad's gun cabinet. He took out a gun and one bullet. He brought the loaded gun to the alley behind our house and then, between our house and the neighbor's house, he took his own life. He aimed the gun directly at his blind eye and shot himself in the face.

The neighbor found him and called the police.

My dad remembers getting the call at work to go home immediately; they didn't tell him much else. By the time he got home, they had already removed Mark's body, but the evidence of what Mark had done was still there. All he could think about was that it had to be cleaned up before we kids got home from school.

My dad recently shared this experience with me. As I brought up the subject, he couldn't even speak for a moment. We both just sat there and silently cried together over our IHOP breakfasts. I can't even imagine what it must have been like for him to have to come home to that horrific scene. He had to process what had just happened while simultaneously dealing with the immediate necessity of preparing for the arrival of the other children – to clean up the alley. Mark was my dad's stepson; my dad had been the father figure in Mark's life for 10 years – the hardest, yet most rewarding, years. And then he was gone. What an overwhelming burden to not only shoulder this grief but to somehow be there for the rest of the family in their grief. Unimaginable guilt must have taken hold, knowing that it was his gun that Mark used. Even though the guns were locked away, Mark had been able to take one. My God, my poor dad!

He doesn't even remember coming to the school with my aunt to get me and the twins that day. I was in 3rd grade. I remember being called to the principal's office over the loudspeaker. I remember hearing some of the kids in my class calling out, "Ooooooh, someone's in trouble!" But I was a good kid; I couldn't think of what I could have possibly done to merit a trip to the principal's office.

As I walked into the office, my dad was sitting there, and I could tell something was very wrong. It was just the two of us. I think my aunt was getting the twins. He sat me on his lap and told me that Mark was gone, that he was dead. I don't remember anything else he said. He sobbed and cried on my shoulder like he was the child, and I held him as I cried too. I don't know if I even understood the enormity of what he had just told me, but I understood how devastated my dad was. His devastation filled the entire room, and I very clearly felt it. I think that's why I was crying; I could feel my dad's pain.

The days and weeks after this moment are a blur. The intensity of the emotions was so heavy in the house that I went back to school the next day. I didn't have to go, but I chose to go. Of course, I wasn't at all ready to be there or to face the flood of questions that came at me, but I think it was easier than being at home.

I don't think younger kids rely as much on the spoken language as adults do. It seems strange because it's not something we really tend to discuss. When we are younger, before we learn to talk, we have to communicate non-verbally. We are experts at reading body language, sounds, and facial cues. I also think that children can read and feel the energy around them, kind of like animals would. It's a natural process that phases out as we get older and more dependent on words to communicate. Children are very tuned in to emotional energy because they don't have a spoken language yet. At the time of Mark's death, I had been talking for 7 years, but I think that the skill of reading a room is still very sharp at that young age.

I don't think that I had any understanding of the finality of death. I knew Mark wasn't coming back, but the idea of death eluded me. For me, it was as though he had moved away. I also hadn't yet been programmed about death, so I didn't really have any thoughts or feelings about it. Because of this, I was in pretty good shape; I wasn't grieving. I still had an untainted inner awareness that the spirit of my brother was still very much alive and well somewhere. My own outward emotions were nothing more than me mirroring the magnitude of sadness I felt around me. The grief that permeated my family paralyzed me. I think this is where most of my own sadness stemmed from.

Through my journey, as I have processed Mark's death, I've realized that this is possibly an occurrence or experience where we are taught to hold on to: to feel pain for those passing through our lives. Not just for the ones that pass away, but also for the ones still living. We grieve people who are still alive when they depart from our lives, rather than letting them flow through freely; we do not allow ourselves to be at peace with it. Is this where we learn to fear change and death?

It seems we are taught to feel loss because someone is gone, rather than to appreciate having had them in our lives to begin with. I say I was taught this because I remember my natural instinct was to talk about Mark and celebrate him, but the reactions of the people around me said that this approach was inappropriate. Maybe it was because of how he died and the stigma around suicide at the time. I didn't understand why everyone was so sad. He was in what most people call Heaven! In my mind, what could be better?

Unfortunately for my mom, her Catholic upbringing told her that Mark was sent to Hell, where his soul would be tortured for eternity because he committed suicide. This idea, and what my mother went through, still makes me sick to my stomach. I do not believe this, on any level, and I never have. Even at the young age of 8, in my heart, I knew better. There is absolutely no possible way that my creator would ever send someone to endure eternal damnation because they were too sad to exist in this world. I don't even believe in a place called Hell. Maybe "Hell" is an existence that is created in one's mind, based on thoughts and experiences someone is going through, but it's not eternal. It cannot be eternal because nothing remains the same.

The only trip to Hell my brother experienced was when he was here, on Earth. It took place in his human mind and body. The depression he experienced and the actions he took came out of the grief that he felt for the life he had before his accident. He was grieving a part of himself that was forever changed. He was grieving the loss of who he had been and a life where he felt whole. He was grieving the loss of connection he had felt in his friendships. A part of my brother died in that accident and a new aspect of himself showed up, and he didn't know who he was anymore or how he fit into the world. Instead of continuously working on acclimating and integrating that new aspect of himself, he chose to follow the part of himself that had already left.

If anyone spent any time in Hell after Mark's suicide, it was my mom. As a mother myself, I cannot even begin to imagine what my mom was going through. One of her children was too sad to continue existing and took his own life; as a mother, how do you deal with that? The inevitable sense of loss and failure would be enough to send any mother into her own personal Hell. But on top of that, her religion was telling her that Mark would be eternally punished for this brief act. There would be no love or healing for her child from God. Can you even begin to imagine the grief and powerlessness she must have felt losing a child to suicide because he was too sad? Or guilt that she should have seen it coming, or that she should have done more? Or the hopelessness she must have felt regarding her God, her Father, her Protector, her Savior, the being who was supposed to love us the most, unconditionally, sending her child, who was sick and in so much mental anguish that he didn't want to live anymore, to Hell? If there is a place called Hell, my mom was going through it.

I had wanted to talk about Mark's death. I had questions. I wanted to understand why Mark died, but the emotions were so intense around me that there was no one to talk to about it. My mom's demeanor was unrecognizable to me. Looking back, she may have been heavily medicated to get through it.

In the days after, she was surrounded by family and friends trying to support her. I felt like an outsider trying to see what was happening in the center of the crowd, trying to make it to the front row of the show but being pushed back by security. Catching glimpses of my mom, but not really getting to connect with her. I don't think she was capable of connecting with anything at that point anyway. The fact that she was still breathing was enough and all she could manage, I'm sure.

I remember the day of the funeral. My mom is really the only person I have any memory of that day. I remember being at the funeral home and then the cemetery, but she is the only person I remember any details about. She tried so hard to go into the room where Mark's casket was, but in every attempt, she ended up in the bathroom throwing up instead. I remember going back and forth, from checking on my mom, to greeting people as they came into the funeral home. I took it upon myself to be the welcoming committee; that's who I was. I walked up to his casket on several occasions to be a witness to others paying their respects. I tried to comfort those who were crying. Even then, I was trying to shine my light into a very dark situation.

I don't really remember anything else after the funeral. My mom spent a lot of time in her room with the door shut. My dad seemed to just disappear. We kids tiptoed around in silence through the heaviness for a while. We didn't talk about it. It was too painful for my mom.

There's a healthy way of dealing with something and moving forward, and then there is sweeping something under the carpet and moving forward. We did the latter. We all just shut down, pretended we were ok, and kind of acted like it never happened. It was like everyone just forgot about him.

I remember a time later, I said something to my mom about Mark, and she acted like she didn't know who I was talking about. I think she actually said, " I don't know who you are talking about." She acted like she never had a son named Mark. I was so confused! Much later, when I was in my 30's, she told me her grief was too much, and she couldn't cope. For a time, the only way she made it through was to literally pretend he never existed.

Going through counseling, I have learned a lot about what I carried with me from this trauma. My thoughts, beliefs, and patterning were all impacted. I can look back on my life and very clearly see the effects. This is what that 8-year-old little girl picked up from that experience and took with her for the rest of her life, until last year.

We hide our grief. We don't talk about it. We say we are okay, even if we aren't. When things are too emotionally painful to handle, we pretend it never happened. We bury it. We don't talk about things that make other people feel uncomfortable.

Understanding how my family's grieving process impacted my coping mechanisms, I have a much, much better awareness of how I was able to keep every subsequent trauma I endured buried so well for so long.

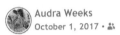

Audra Weeks
October 1, 2017 ·

I went to visit where my brother Mark is buried yesterday. This is 1 of 5 traumas I'm working through currently.
He took his own life when I was 8. His passing was my first experience with death.
As you can imagine because of his age and how he exited there was a lot of trauma in the house. My mom's religion also taught that suicides went to hell. (How incredibly fucked up!) I remember a few weeks of chaos and then things quieted down and it was like it never happened.
I believe there was an unbearable suffering in silence happening and a lot behind closed doors. Maybe it was hidden from me because I was so young? As a mom, I can not even begin to imagine.
A belief I took away from this was, we are supposed to hide our grief and pain and say we are ok even if we aren't, especially if it's going to upset someone else.
I've been doing this my whole life through experiences that no one would be "ok" with.
In counseling I've come to realize that I also carry guilt and sadness that it was like we all just forgot him.
I'm not one that believes you need to go to a grave to commune. I believe Mark is every-where and in all things because his energy is with the Creative energy of all things.
I felt a need to physically do something to acknowledge his existence. To acknowledge he was here. So, I just went and sat there in silence. It was a lot more emotional than I thought it was going to be.
I also have a lot of sadness because of lack of memory on my part. He was 10yrs older than me so, he was High School age and wasn't around much. Maybe friends or family members that knew him could share a memory to help me remember and celebrate him?
Thank you all for sharing his healing journey with me. I AM grateful!
PEACE and LOVE

 87   57 Comments

CHAPTER 9

COLLATERAL BEAUTY

PART 1

And perhaps
what made her beautiful was not her appearance or
what she achieved, but in her love
and in her courage and her audacity to believe;
no matter the darkness around her,
Light ran wild within her,
and that was the way she came alive,
and it showed up in everything.

~Morgan Harper Nichols

*I*f I've learned anything from having experienced trauma and some pretty tough situations, it's that there is always collateral beauty. In a traumatic situation, we are so often caught up in what happened to us – the story. Or we are stuck in the tougher emotions around it, such as fear, guilt, shame, anger, resentment, and grief. We miss the collateral beauty.

I promise you it's there.

We miss it because, in order to see it, we have to allow ourselves to open up to all the possibilities of the situation. We actually have to sit with what happened and really dig into how we feel about it. We have to take it apart, turn it over, and analyze it. It means working through the uncomfortable parts; seeing it all the way through. Believe it or not, an awful experience might have something meaningful to teach you. It might actually have something good to offer your life. It can even enhance your life in some way if you allow it to.

I'm all about finding collateral beauty. I'll be gosh-darned if I'm going to go through something hard and not have something good to take away from it! Sometimes I see it right away, or it may be months or even years later, but it's there. I would like to share with you some collateral beauty around my brother, Mark. It's actually how I got the title for my book.

⌒

When I started writing this book, my perfectionism had me a little hung up, because I didn't have a title. It took a lot for me to just start writing and let go of not having a title and allowing that to come when the time was right. I'm chuckling, because if somehow I could let you see into my process and how orderly it needs to be, you'd probably chuckle too! I think having order is part of how I am managing my emotions while writing. If I can keep things neat, tidy, and in order, I can create an illusion of control. I'm all over anything that allows me to think I am able to keep the unmanageable, manageable. I'm still learning that life is not always, nor does it need to be, manageable.

When I was approaching the beginnings of the chapter "Mark", I had no idea how to start. I knew I wanted to honor him and those in despair. I wanted to tell you all about him, with the opportunity for you to catch even a glimpse of who he was, what he went through, and what happened to my family and my own journey as a result. I wanted to write it all in a way that would be helpful, to bring about healing to all who have experienced anything to do with suicide and loss. Having set such a lofty goal for myself, I felt a lot of pressure.

I began praying. I prayed for GOD, The Universe, to help me open up like a channel to let this chapter, that I believe is already written, in the ethers, to come to me, and through me, out onto the paper. I was praying to be an instrument of service. I was asking Mark to help me help others and honor him. I was asking him what he would want, and how he would like his chapter to be written. I prayed and meditated for a couple of weeks before I ever wrote a single word.

In the meantime, my boss, Lisa, was reading a book by Rachel Hollis. She was so excited about this book! She couldn't wait to finish it so she could share it with me. When I began reading it, I connected with the author right away. Her brother had committed suicide too. I could definitely see where Lisa's excitement was coming from.

Rachel Hollis had created a documentary as well, and it just so happened that it was playing in the movie theater right down the street for one night. That's weird! I've never even heard of a one-night-only documentary at a movie theater. And what were the odds of this kind of timing anyway?

Lisa, with her super huge heart and her excitement about Rachel, bought tickets for herself, me, and a few others. In the documentary, Rachel talked in more detail about her brother and how he committed suicide. It turns out that he did the same thing my brother did. I cried through at least half of that documentary. I connected with this much more than I connected with her book. There were some points where I actually held my breath to contain the ugly cries that wanted to burst forth!

Rachel talked about putting in the work to make your dreams come true. The example she used a lot of the time was writing, because that's what she had experience with. Well, I was writing a book, so I could relate to everything she said on a personal level. Are you beginning to see things unfolding here? Literally, her path wasn't just an example to me. It was real! Everything she was saying, word-for-word, was a mirror to my own experience because her example was my real life. I swear, she was talking directly to me. It was insanely cool!

~

I couldn't thank Lisa enough for sharing this with me. I couldn't put into words exactly how much gratitude I had. I knew something profound had just happened.

The next day, Lisa sent a link with the Top 10 Takeaways of Rachel's documentary. I could relate to many of them, but the last one was like a gold nugget. I remember hearing Rachel talk about "moving mountains" to make your dreams come true. This particular detail clearly needed to be brought to my attention again, because it was important. The Top 10 Takeaways brought it to light again by restating the words, "moving mountains". There it was. The minute I saw the printed words, I knew it was the title of my book.

~

I reached out to my son, Chandler, immediately because I knew there was a bible verse about it. With all the praying I had been doing, I wanted to know what that verse was. I knew Jesus had talked about moving mountains in a metaphorical sense and I love metaphors! I also felt that moving mountains was the perfect metaphor for working through trauma. Was there a message there for me? I was beyond ecstatic and I had to know more!

Chandler is very biblical in a lot of his beliefs, so he was my go-to on bible information. I told him the beautiful story of how I had come to the title of my book and how I had been praying to GOD and to

Mark and meditating a lot about my 'Mark' chapter. I asked him if he knew the verse I was talking about. He said, "Yes, and Mom, you are not going to believe what book it's in. It's in the book of Mark!" Coincidence? I think not! I. WAS. BAWLING!!!

As you've probably noticed, I use a quote at the beginning of every chapter. I thought that maybe this was an answer to some of my prayers... a quote to help me finally get started writing on the chapter 'Mark'.

> *"Truly I tell you, if anyone says to this mountain, 'Go throw yourself into the sea,' and does not doubt in their heart but believes that what they say will happen, it will be done for them."*

> -Mark 11:23

After much thought, I realized that this series of events wasn't presenting me with the quote for the chapter. It was actually Mark's way of showing me that the title of my book was coming from him.

This gift was beautifully orchestrated through Lisa, Rachel, and Chandler, and was Mark's way of letting me know that he was ultimately the source. There is just no way that that verse about moving mountains was just coincidentally in the book of Mark. No way!

As I read this verse again, I note that I have been doing a lot of thinking about and practicing on manifestation. I'm wondering why some are so great at it, but I seem to be on the struggle bus about it.

Ironically, this whole story on collateral beauty is about belief, faith, and how I came to manifest it for the title of my book, and get myself re-focused on my goal. But in this moment I am gently reminded that, in order to manifest, we have to believe fully that what we are calling forth will come to pass. It may not come exactly how, when, or where we think it will, but it will come! I prayed for help and guidance from my brother, fully believing he would come through, and he did. What he gave me wasn't the opening quote or the spilling-forth of the chapter, as I had imagined, but what did come was the title of my book. That is huge!

This experience was beyond profound. There is no way to capture with words what I experienced and how I felt. I literally felt like I was connected with the universe – that I was sitting in the lap of the creator of all things. I was high on life for a good three days from this experience.

I've experienced much collateral beauty from Mark's death. A little realization here, a boost of strength there, a reminder to embrace the negative in order to experience the positive. And then this one. Although this nugget of collateral beauty came 39 years later, it came. And it was powerful.

For the first time since the passing of my brother, I felt completely connected to him. I genuinely believe he spoke to me from beyond the grave.

CHAPTER 10

STOLEN INNOCENCE

*There are wounds that never show on the body that are deeper and
more hurtful than anything that bleeds.*

~Laurell K. Hamilton

When I was in 5th grade, I contracted mononucleosis ("mono") and was extremely sick for weeks. Soon my mom got it, most likely from me. However, her symptoms were much different than mine were, and she was sick for much longer – for what seemed like months. She battled these mono-like symptoms on and off for three years before she was finally diagnosed with Chronic Fatigue Syndrome (CFS). CFS is stress-related – the more stress, the worse the physical symptoms. CFS can also cause depression, which also gets worse when stress is higher. CFS does not go away and cannot be cured. Even if you are feeling well, CFS is lingering, waiting for your next bout with stress. This becomes important to my story, because I was the one who brought mono to my mother. Logically, I know I bear no blame, but I could not help but feel responsible for her ongoing health issues.

In junior high, although my mom had recently remarried, I had too much freedom and virtually no parental guidance. I was still a "good kid", but I experimented with pot and alcohol a couple of times.

Some might consider the extent of my experiences nothing more than youthful indulgence, but perhaps it started me down a dangerous path.

I had a new father figure in my life and three new stepsiblings. My stepdad had a daughter who was a few years older than I was and two younger sons. One of the boys was just a year younger and the other, about three years younger. They didn't live with us. His daughter came by on occasion, and his boys visited a few times a month.

In 8th grade, I struck up a friendship with one of the girls on my soccer team. She was already in high school, and I was eager to impress the cool, older girl. Inevitably, I got into trouble when I was around her. I didn't want her to think I was uncool, so I followed her lead. But I was also very uncomfortable with the choices I was making. It was not natural for me to be such a rebel; I was mostly a rule-follower. Finally, after we were caught stealing makeup at Gemco, my mom put an end to that friendship. Of course, at the time I pitched a fit, but secretly I was glad she stepped in as the strict parent. I not only needed stability and guidance but I also no longer wanted to feel that peer pressure from my friend.

Life was good. I liked my new stepdad (let's call him "S"), things at home were stable, and I was looking forward to a fun summer before high school began. I was headed to the same high school my siblings went to, and I was excited to begin following in their young-adult footsteps.

⁓

Life was good. Until it wasn't. One evening that summer, S and I were sitting on the porch chatting when I noticed his hard penis coming out of his shorts. It was the 80's, and the short cut-off Levi's were the fashion, and he clearly wasn't wearing any underwear. I was so mortified and embarrassed! Other than maybe a picture of a Greek statue in a history book, I had never seen an adult penis before. I tried to pretend I hadn't seen it, but he knew I had. He so obviously intended for me to see it. I was so repulsed! Even now, writing about it, I can feel that same revulsion. I actually feel sick to my stomach.

S then proceeded to describe his perverse feelings toward me. He informed me that when he was having sex with my mom, it was me he thought about. He also told me he thought about me when he was in the shower.

I was barely 14 years old! I felt incredibly unsafe, and it made me feel dirty! To have a grown man who was supposed to be a father figure discussing sex, while his erect penis hung out of his shorts was indescribably disgusting! I didn't say anything. I was paralyzed with fear, but I instinctively got up as fast as I could and went into the house. He lived here too! Where could I go to be safe in my own house? I went into the family room, where one of the twins was watching TV, and I sat in there with him. I was naive and terrified. I didn't know what to do; I was in total shock.

After a few minutes, S appeared in the family room. My heart stopped. I couldn't breathe. He asked, and then pleaded with me to come talk to him. There was just no way in hell that was going to happen, obviously. I had no intention of going anywhere near him.

I told S, quite firmly, to leave me alone. He did. He left the room, and I sat there in sheer panic. Of course, I didn't have the first clue how to handle this. I was worried that my brother would leave the room and I'd be left alone, defenseless. I was too embarrassed and humiliated to tell my brother or anyone what I had just experienced. The one man in my life whose role was to protect me had exposed his erect penis while telling me he fantasized about me during sex with my mom. How was I supposed to tell anyone that!?

I wonder what my brother was thinking. Could he have had any idea what was happening? It's strange for me to think back on it and realize that my brother was completely oblivious to the experience I had just had. He had no idea how scared I was. He had no idea that his presence was the only safety I felt in that moment. He just sat there and watched T.V. while I experienced something that would impact me for the rest of my life. What a surreal recognition.

—

I avoided S at all costs for a few days. I didn't even go home. It was summer, so making plans to be out of the house or at my friend's was an easy enough task. I ended up telling the whole thing to my best friend at the time, Stacy. This was something I could not carry by myself. It was a huge burden, and I was scared to be home. I didn't feel safe there anymore, not even in my own room with the door locked.

Stacy encouraged me to tell my mom, but that just didn't feel like an option for me. I had seen enough after school specials where the mom didn't believe the child, sometimes even blamed the child. Besides, how on Earth was I supposed to tell my mom that her husband displayed his penis to me, or that he fantasized about me during sex with her? I felt ashamed, like it was my fault. I didn't even understand any of it. How was I supposed to communicate this to her?

Thank goodness Stacy had enough sense to go to her mom about it. The situation was just way too big for two 14-year-olds to handle, and she knew it. We needed an adult to help us sort it out. I needed an adult. I needed an adult to be on my side, both figuratively and literally.

Stacy's mom sat me down, and together we talked about it. I felt so relieved when we talked. She reassured me that no part of it was my fault. Her words brought me a lot of comfort until she told me that we had to tell my mom. She reassured me and told me that she would be with me, that I wouldn't be alone. I was still reluctant to go to my mom. I don't know why I was worried. My mom could be strict and no-nonsense, but she wasn't a scary person. I guess I didn't know how to approach her. For whatever reason, I thought she would be mad at me. Plus, I had been trained to keep uncomfortable stuff to myself, to shoulder emotional burdens alone, in silence. Or maybe I didn't want to be the reason my mom's world fell apart again.

Stacy's mom called my mom; we were all to meet at Bob's Big Boy. Stacy's mom and I arrived first; we sat at a table and waited for my mom. The apprehension was killing me.

It was clear that my mom had been crying when she approached the table. She knew. When she had mentioned to S that she was meeting with me and my friend's mom to talk about something important, he knew he was about to be outed. So he told her. Now, as an adult, I am really glad he had the courage to tell her. It would have been over-the-top awful for my mom to have been completely blind-sided by another parent about what was happening to her daughter in her own house.

The conversation went much differently than I had imagined. I had been worried that my mom would be angry with me, but she had no anger, and she believed everything I had to say. I remember crying a lot, and my shame and extreme discomfort made it difficult for me to describe what had happened. I'm sure that S's pre-emptive confession helped my mom accept what I was saying.

I had just turned 14 and was getting ready to start my first year of high school. This should have been a carefree time – a new, adventurous beginning. I was an innocent. I had never even French-kissed a boy. I was a freckle-faced redhead with no sexual experience. Yet here I was, forced to have a conversation about very disturbing adult matters.

While I worked on this chapter, I kept trying to understand why so many young girls and women blame themselves in this type of situation. Why on Earth did I feel ashamed? It wasn't my fault; clearly, I had done nothing wrong. Where does that self-blame even come from?

I can't really remember the time line of how the details unfolded, but the agreement was that S would go to counseling and that if anything ever happened again, my mom would leave him – no ifs, and's, or buts.

⌒

My mom tried to have some conversations with me about it at first, but I wasn't really open to it. For me, it didn't matter how I was really feeling about it all. I just wanted to sweep it all under the rug and move on as fast as I possibly could, as I had been trained to do. It was such an uncomfortable and humiliating situation for me that discussing it was just too painful. I trusted the adults to manage the details; I wanted to be left out of it. And so we all moved on and pretended it never happened. At the time, this was fine with me!

The truth of the matter was, that I was not fine, not at all. Prior to this, I had actually really liked S. He was a very kind, caring, and big-hearted person. It felt nice to have a father figure present in my life daily who wanted to talk to me. He was interested in hearing about my day or whatever I was excited about. He listened to me and wanted to spend time with me. I hadn't had that before; it was a big deal to me. S had made me feel special, like I mattered. And then he destroyed it. Not only did he ruin our relationship, but he contributed to my warped understanding of what a relationship with a man should be. This is when I started to equate men's abusive behavior with love, thereby giving men permission to walk all over me.

⌒

As a child, my peers didn't appreciate my freckles and red hair, but older people, men especially, always told me how beautiful I was, and how stunning my hair was. After S's verbal sexual assault, I hated hearing these compliments from men. It terrified me. It triggered me deeply. I was sure they all wanted to molest me. It was awful!

I was still completely uncomfortable being in the same room with S, and I refused to be for a very long time. Every time I saw him going to take a shower, my stomach turned and knotted up, remembering what he had told me. Despite the promises, I didn't feel safe in my own home. He avoided me and I, him. It was a very tense, anxious existence.

Somewhere in all of this, my mom had found out that this was not his first issue with this type of behavior. Because of what happened with me, she started asking questions and found that he had molested his own daughter for years. She was two or three years older than I was. He still had a relationship with her, so my mom hadn't realized that anything was off. It turns out that he and his daughter had gone to counseling and salvaged part of their relationship. She was not around much, but what teenager with a driver's license hangs out with her parents? No red flags were raised.

Obviously, my family wasn't the only one that harbored dark secrets.

⌒

It is especially tragic that his family knew all this when he met my mom. They also knew that she had a teen-aged daughter, and yet they said nothing. His family threw me to the wolves rather than acknowledge the problem.

All of this backstory about S's past is something I learned as an adult. Part of me is really glad that I didn't know any of this when

S and my mom were still together, because I was already scared and uncomfortable. If I had known that he had molested his own child, it would have been impossible for me to live under the same roof. Even without this information, I was mystified as to how my mom could have stayed with him after what he did to me. But she knew that he was capable of much worse, and she *still* stayed. If I had known about her choice then, I would have questioned whether she had my back at all.

Even now, her choice is a difficult one for me to understand. How could my mom stay in a relationship that continued to put her child in the way of physical and emotional harm? What was going on with her that she would even *want* to stay with a man who had those kinds of issues? My best guess is that she thought she could fix him.

⌒

Early in this marriage, I had gotten along well with S's sons. But after the incident, it was very uncomfortable when they came over to visit. I'm sure they perceived my behavior as distant and aloof. They may have thought I was just a spoiled brat. Little did they know that I was shouldering a terrible secret about their dad.

As I started my freshman year, my relationship with S had been effectively destroyed, and I of course began to disconnect from him. Unfortunately, since S and my mom still had a relationship, that meant disconnecting from her as well. She was sick all the time. She and S had begun building a house, which was hugely stressful. She was trying to save her marriage. I was not seeking her guidance as a parent, either because of what had transpired or as part of normal adolescent distancing. Probably a little of both. I was starting to participate in risky behaviors, but no one was really paying any attention to what I was doing. Much of my behavior was classic attention-seeking and a cry for help, but no one noticed. Unfortunately, I was an expert at creating a facade, and pretty good at keeping secrets, so I did a decent job of hiding my emotional state and anything that might get me in trouble from my mom.

Other than the couple mistakes I had made in 8th grade, I was a really good kid. I had a pretty solid head on my shoulders and for the most part, made pretty good decisions. My mom had no reason to think anything was any different. About midway through freshman year, I started making choices that reflected a lack of direction and a lack of self-esteem. At this point, my mom seemed to have checked out. After a long road of being sick, she had finally been diagnosed with Chronic Fatigue Syndrome. She now knew what she was dealing with, but she would have to endure a lifetime of stress-induced fatigue and debilitating depression. In my head, this was my fault, since I brought the mono home. So, disconnected from parental influence, having no real guidance, with a willingness to take unwise risks, and a warped sense of relationships, I ventured forth.

I was making some pretty poor choices by the end of my freshman year that got worse throughout high school. Some choices were probably normal exploration, but I didn't have anyone really parenting me at this point, so I was never redirected off that rocky path.

I did have my older siblings. I idolized them, and they were a huge influence. Although they never pushed anything on me, I knew they were all pretty experienced when it came to drugs and their choices. This was the direction I headed. So now, I'm a naive risk-taker with no real guidance, seeking approval while confused about what approval looks like. No one is available to guide me or protect me.

As an adult, I can look back on my stepdad, S, and know, there was something wrong with him. He was sick. There is something sick if an adult desires physical intimacy with a child. A child, of course, doesn't even know about physical intimacy or what it means. There is definitely something mental going on in the mind of the adult if this is where their thoughts are leading them. Although S had been called out, and had promised to leave me alone, he could not escape his nature.

⌁

A year and a half had gone by since that day on the porch. My mom and S had begun building a house in New River, about 40 minutes north of our house in Phoenix. It was seriously in the middle of nowhere! There were other people living out there, but it was very rural and spread out with a totally different culture of people.

Building the house had taken a financial toll, so they sold the house in town to finance the construction. Now there was no house for any of us to live in. My mom and S moved out to New River and camped on the lot while they built the house. I moved in with my best friend, Tammy, and her mom in Phoenix. They had an extra room and happily took me in so I could live in a home while I finished my sophomore year. Living with them was a much-needed respite. I was finally living in a stable home without having to go to great lengths to avoid S.

⌁

After finishing my sophomore year, I too moved out to the house in New River. This would be my home now. I rejoined my family and would attend the local high school in the fall. I hated it! I had lived in the same home for my entire life until I moved in with Tammy and her mom. My friends were in town. I was part of the culture there. Everything I'd ever known was there.

The town of New River and the people in it were an absolute culture shock to me. These were country folk, and I was a city girl. They wore cowboy boots, drove dusty trucks, and seemed to have their own language. The closest grocery store was 30 minutes away. The house, which wasn't even completed, was on a dirt road. I had no friends, and everything I knew was nearly an hour away. It was unbearably isolating.

That summer I was conscripted as an unpaid construction worker to help finish the house. In my free time, I took long walks; during these walks, I smoked a lot of pot. Usually, it was pot that I had taken from my mom's stash.

At this point, 2 years after the porch incident, there was some communication between me and S. Enough time had passed with no issues that I was feeling much more comfortable, and I was trying to build a civil relationship with him. After all, we still lived in the same house. I'm sure I was a total pain in the ass though. I had become unruly over the last year, and I was angry. I was angry that my mom made the choice to move us out to no man's land. I was angry that I had to do manual labor and live in a house that barely had water and electricity. I was grieving the life and friends I had lost by moving. And I was apprehensive about starting a new school with a bunch of country folk with whom I had nothing in common. Yeah, I'm sure I was an absolute joy to live with.

Even at 16, I wasn't one to judge the lifestyles of people who were different than I was, so I could be friends with anyone. I was easygoing enough that the other juniors seemed to have no trouble accepting me. But, as anyone who has been through high school can attest, fitting in is key. It's one thing to have someone to eat lunch with, but what I really craved was a group of friends to which I could belong. Junior year was probably one of the more challenging years of my life. I did have trouble fitting in with my peers in New River.

In desperation, I ended up making some poor choices. It seems as though every high school has a "Stoner" group. City, country, and every school in between, there is always a group of kids who would rather hang out and get high than just about anything else. The Stoners were much more my speed than, say, the "Cowboys", with whom I had nothing in common. And, true to their name, the Stoners, and I, did drugs. As part of this social group, I spent my weekends drinking and smoking weed. I actually didn't even like drinking. I hated the taste of beer, but I did it anyway, to fit in and to seem cool. As part of my unwritten social contract with this group, I started experimenting with some heavier drugs.

One friend I did have in New River was my stepbrother, SB. I would say he was my best friend, as a matter of fact. That friendship really evolved when he and I both moved out to New River to our parents' new house. We were both starting a brand new high school and knew no one but each other, so we were all each other had. I deeply valued and appreciated him, especially during this difficult time!

Another friend I was fortunate to have was David. I think David had fallen in love with me when I first moved to New River. Everyone knew he liked me. I knew it, and friends had tried to get me to go out with him, but I never did. He was a couple years older than I was, and well-liked. No one messed with David; I felt safe when I was with him. Even though his life was a bit of a mess, I knew he genuinely cared about me. We were very good friends, and he always looked out for me.

One Friday night, my mom was in Mexico, and SB was in town at his mom's. I was hanging out at David's house. He and I had stayed up most of the night partying, and by Saturday morning I was wiped out. I went home to my mom's empty house to sleep for a while and then to shower and get ready for Saturday night.

I woke up later in the afternoon to see my stepdad in my room. He was standing over my bed, watching me sleep. What in the actual fuck!? I could smell the whiskey on his breath. I was angry, and I was scared he was there. This was not a good situation and I knew it! Completely freaked out, I yelled at him to get out of my room. He said he was lonely with my mom and his son gone, and he just wanted someone to talk to. He was clearly very drunk, and yelling at him to get out was having no effect. To delay any further interaction, I told him that I would come talk to him for a while after I took a shower. That worked and he finally left my room.

Of course, I had no intention of staying there. I got up and locked my bedroom and bathroom doors and showered and got ready as fast as I could. Hoping he was too drunk to notice, I tried to sneak out to my car.

But he was there, outside, waiting for me. Panicked, I could feel myself shaking. I was alone.

There was nowhere I could run. Calling out for help would be useless. How was I going to get to my car, get in, and lock the door before he got to me?

I made a dash for it.

I didn't make it.

He got in between me and my car and wouldn't let me leave. He stood there, reminding me that I promised I would talk to him after I got ready. I tried to breezily tell him that I changed my mind and that I had to leave. He was persistent, so I demanded that he get out of my way so I could leave. His tone was pleading, cajoling, as he begged me to stay and talk, but his body language was aggressive. He stood firm and would not let me leave.

Then he started to bargain with me. He would let me leave if I let him kiss me. I felt my adrenaline soar out of fear. Terrified, I pushed past him and ran for my car. He grabbed me by my jacket, pulling me back. I wriggled out of the jacket as he pulled on it, and shoved him backward, making another dash for my car. Thank GOD I had the keys in my hand and not in my jacket pocket!

I got in, slammed the door shut and locked it. I was crying, terrified, and in shock, but I was safe in my car. With my jacket in his hands, he stood there behind my car, smirking. He thought he had trapped me by standing behind the car. He realized very quickly that I was willing to run him over to get out of there. This time, I won!

$\frown$

I stayed that night at David's. I didn't go home until Sunday when I knew SB would be back from Phoenix. SB could tell from the way I was acting that something was wrong. I stuck to SB like his shadow; wherever he went, I followed. If SB got up to get a snack, I followed him to the kitchen.

If he went outside, I was right there with him. If he went to the bathroom, I was waiting outside the door. Obviously, he was concerned and wanted to know what was going on. Without giving him all the history, I caved and told him what had happened over the weekend. He was devastated to hear that his father had done this to me, and he was very concerned for me and my well-being.

SB and I were sitting at the kitchen table as my stepdad came downstairs and sat down. SB was seething. I thought he was going to kill S. He was furious! SB's whole chest was beet red and his fists were clenched. He confronted S through his clenched teeth, telling him not to speak to me or even look at me. I was glad that SB was standing up for me, but it was awful to see what he was going through. I felt awful for him, having to come face-to-face with this dark side of his own father. He was in shock, devastated.

My mom got home the next day. Those old worries about what to tell my mother about her husband cropped up again: would she believe me? Would she be mad at me? But I remembered that, after S's first assault, she *did* believe me, and was genuinely concerned for me. I told her what he did. To my great relief, she believed me again. And she remembered her promise from two years earlier: she told him the marriage was over. Of course, he got defensive and tried to explain his behavior away as a misunderstanding, but she held firm. Their discussion got more and more heated. He had been drinking and was belligerent. As he came to realize the finality of my mom's decision, he turned violent. When he pulled out a shotgun, we decided to leave and call the police. They came and saw he was sitting on the porch with a shotgun, somehow saw nothing wrong with this, and did absolutely nothing to help us.

The next day, after S went to work, my mom took back control and occupancy of the house and had an order of protection served on him.

I don't know enough to give you details about how their relationship ended. I don't know if it was amicable after that, or if it continued to be a battle between them. I let my mom handle it and I checked out of all of it. All I knew was that I never had to see him again. As illogical as it seems, I added the burden of my mom's third failed marriage to my emotional load.

I moved forward with my own life, pretending I was tough as nails, while my life choices got worse and worse.

CHAPTER 11

NO CONSENT

Now, every time I witness a strong person, I want to know:
What darkness did you conquer in your story? Mountains do
not rise without earthquakes.

~Katherine Mackenett

he rest of my junior year and into my senior year was an absolute shit show! I found myself drinking my way into oblivion on the weekends, at desert parties, frequently. Good Ole Jungle Juice to the rescue! I was smoking pot often. I had started dabbling in heavier drugs like crystal meth, acid, and mushrooms on occasion. I had also become very promiscuous. Promiscuity turned out to be the most damaging thing I was doing to myself. It definitely caused me the most inner pain.

During this time, my mom seemed to have completely checked out again. Her husband's assault on me and the subsequent divorce proceedings caused her chronic fatigue to skyrocket. She was sick and in bed often, so she had no idea what was going on with her newly rebellious, promiscuous daughter. Even if she had known, I don't think she had it in her to be the mother I needed at that time. The only thing she knew for sure was that I was starting to fail my classes. That detail of my life was the only thing I couldn't hide from her.

My relationship with her became very strained. We fought a lot. She was trying to be a mom with only a small window into my world. I thought I was more mature than I was, and I was slipping through her fingers. She would ground me, and I would just sneak out my window. My will to self-destruct was definitely much stronger than her ability to contain me.

I felt that I was being forced to live in a world she had chosen for herself, and I hated her for it. I hated her for moving me out to New River. I hated who I was becoming in an attempt to fit in. I hated what I had gone through with my stepdad. She had made a mistake in choosing him for a husband, and it had cost me too much! This place, my new school, these people, and even her worsened CFS, were all the result of her choices, and *her* choices were why I was in this situation.

For the record, I don't have any ill will towards my mom anymore. We actually became really close later in life. As an adolescent, of course, I didn't really have any awareness beyond myself and what I was experiencing. In reality, none of this was her fault; it was just life happening. We were both doing the best we could with it all, armed with what we knew at the time, which is all any of us can do.

Ironically, I also felt guilty. My mom's ship seemed to be sinking, and I was blaming myself. I told myself that I was the reason her third marriage failed, and therefore I was the reason for her ill health.

⌒

I have no idea why I've always felt I've needed to shoulder the blame. Looking back, I see myself doing that a lot. Maybe it stemmed from my brother's suicide and being told to be quiet so I didn't make it harder for my mom. But, seeing that her grief persisted, I blamed myself for not adhering to that command. This feeling may have been compounded when my mom and dad were going through their break up – my mom's second divorce. There was a lot of fighting about money and child support – my support. It was a big deal to my dad, and he brought it up for years even after he didn't have to pay it any more. He was very resentful about it, and I felt like he resented me, like I was nothing more than a burden. At least part of me felt I was unwanted by him, blamed by him. Somewhere in there is the origin of my need to carry a burden alone, even when it wasn't mine to carry.

In New River, I was lost, completely out of control, and miserable. My failing grades meant that I would attend high school for a fifth year, and I didn't even care. I was just trying to make it through the day. I couldn't see a future for myself, so there was no sense in working toward one.

My promiscuity really began taking a toll on me mentally and emotionally. It felt good to have boys finally appreciating my strawberry-blonde hair. My 'chunkiness' had turned into womanly curves. I felt pretty and desirable for the first time in my life, but it was fragile and shallow. Of course, the boys who were newly-drawn to me were not interested in a real connection. I would feel energized, powerful, and loved during the flirtation, but I was tossed aside when it was all over. Each emotional crash left me feeling unlovable.

Yet this was a choice I had actively made. Earlier, I had actually turned away a young man who had respected me, because I had no idea how to deal with that response from a man. I had already been trained to know that men had little use for women beyond the physical. So when faced with a good-looking, popular, accomplished suitor who treated me well and wanted to connect, what was I to do? Chase him away, obviously. He didn't fit the mold of the path of self-destruction I had already committed to. He didn't validate the awful core beliefs that I had about myself. I genuinely did not know how to be in a healthy relationship. Things may have looked very different for me if I had given that relationship a chance. I really liked him as a person, and we were strongly attracted to one another. If I had been at a point where I could have allowed myself to have some joy, a good relationship could have changed the trajectory of my life. I'm sure I would not have experienced so much trauma if I had been able to let him in my life.

Sometime after Christmas, when I was 17, I attended New River's annual Country Saturday Night. It was a weekend-long party with music, food, kegs of beer, and whatever else people brought. I think everyone in the town of New River and the surrounding area showed up for at least part of it. Country Saturday Night was a very big deal. It was also the dream weekend for kids who liked to party because no one seemed to care what we kids were doing out there.

There were literally hundreds of people there! I went with my best friend, and we met up with our normal group once we got there. The energy was high with the large crowd and the music. There was so much excitement; it was like being at a live outdoor concert. We danced and laughed so much! The party literally lasted all night and into the next day. You could tell who the hard-core partiers were; they were the ones who were still there in the morning. Even though I was pretty hard-core, I wasn't one of those that night. I thought it was going to be one of the most fun nights of my life!

I didn't do anything out of the ordinary that night. I drank and smoked pot. Unfortunately, I drank way more than I normally did. I despised the taste of beer, so I was doing shots — shots of whatever was given to me. Even though they were unpleasant too, doing shots was much easier for me to stomach than beer was.

Needless to say, I drank myself into a stupor. This was, by far, the most drunk I had ever been. I was completely wasted, and it was late. It had to have been after midnight because about half the people had left.

I was in bad shape. My vision was blurred and I thought I was going to be sick. I stumbled over to what I thought was my friend's car, but I honestly don't know whose car it was. I climbed into the back seat and passed out. I have no idea if I even shut the door after I got in. I probably just lay down and died.

Sometime later I was woken by someone lying on top of me. I was still drunk, slipping in and out of consciousness. I remember realizing that this was a guy I went to school with. I realized he was raping me; I could feel that he was inside of me, but there was nothing I could do. I had absolutely no control of my body. In and out of consciousness I went while it was happening. I can remember flashes of his face while he was on top of me, inside of me, the music still playing in the background. Feeling like I was going to throw up. His muffled voice through my drunken haze, or was it a voice? Sounds? Words? Everything was spinning. I shut my eyes, blacked out, and was roused again. Over and over.

I have no idea how long I was in the back seat of that car. I have no idea how long the rape lasted or how long I lay there afterward. At some point, I started sobering up, and I realized that my pants were off. My panties were off. My shoes were off. The door on the side where my feet were, was open. I had been lying in the back seat of a car, completely exposed.

How many people walked by that car and saw me like that? Did anyone walk by while I was being raped? Did anyone think to help me if they did? Did anyone even notice? Did anyone even care?

It was still dark out, but I managed to find my clothes and shoes. Some were on the floor of the car and some on the ground outside of the car. I don't know how, but I got myself dressed. I had my shoes in my hands. Shaking, I walked to the front of the car, and I threw up. I threw up because I was drunk, but I kept throwing up with the realization that I had been raped. When my stomach was empty, I continued dry-heaving until I was exhausted.

Still drunk, I went to look for my friend. I was walking around out there, in the desert, with no shoes on. At some point, my friend and I found each other. The next thing I remember was waking up at home later that morning.

I said nothing about the rape, not even to my best friend. I was ashamed. I was ashamed that I had gotten so drunk that I had absolutely no control of my own body. I thought I got what I deserved because I had been so promiscuous in the past. All I could hear in my head was, "This is your own fault! This is what you get!"

I didn't tell my mom because I had been out doing things I wasn't supposed to be doing. I didn't tell her because I'd be damned if I was going to be the reason, yet again, for her life to spiral downhill. I had watched my mom go through hell and back several times at this point. Heck, I was probably putting her through it already anyway, just by my rebellious behavior. Now, as a mom myself, I know it would be horribly painful to watch one of my kids self-destruct. She was trying to survive and fit into this town too, and there was no way I could drop this on her. I just continued to hear in my head, "This is your own fault! This is what you get!".

The rapist was popular in his group. He was well-known in school and in New River. Who was going to believe me? It didn't matter what the truth was. He would have been looked at like some stud and I would have just been The Slut. Even though I had been out there for almost two years, I was still the new kid on the block. "This is your own fault! This is what you get!"

No. I would, once again, shoulder this on my own. I would bury this as deeply as I could and pretend it never happened.

The rape changed the very core of my being though. Even though I finally started making better choices, and my mom and I started repairing our relationship, it felt like a part of me died that night. There are no words to fully express the depth of the shame I was holding onto.

I withdrew. I didn't want to be physically touched. I closed myself off mentally, emotionally, and spiritually. In my head, I was completely damaged and unloveable. I was ashamed to be seen; I wanted to be invisible.

I avoided the rapist and his group at school. If we crossed paths, I never made eye contact. I rarely went to parties anymore, and I stopped drinking. I hung out with David and his friends a lot. I continued smoking pot and doing meth on occasion, but I didn't go so far as to lose myself anymore.

David and I had continued to be pretty good casual friends, but now we started getting much closer; our relationship grew much deeper. Months after the rape, David and I took our relationship to the next level. We had been friends for two years at this point, so things moved pretty quickly once we made that decision. A few months went by and I found myself pregnant with our daughter, Amber. I quit absolutely every harmful thing I was doing and really tried hard to get it together for her. Having her inside of me made me remember the person I had once been before I had started falling apart. Her essence gave me a new sense of hope and purpose. I had something to live for. David continued to smoke pot on a daily basis, but I totally cleaned up. I moved in with him and finished out my second senior year, ready to pop.

For decades, I told no one what happened to me out at that ballpark. I carried it, along with a tremendous amount of pain and shame, alone. I had done such a good job burying it that sometimes I think I actually forgot about it. But it was always there, affecting my life on a subconscious level.

A couple of years ago, I finally spoke about the rape for the first time in conversation with a friend. It shocked me when I said it out loud. For a moment it was as though I didn't know who was speaking. I felt shame as I recounted the experience, but I also felt relief. After 26 years, I finally verbalized the burden that I had carried alone for so long.

If you have ever experienced anything even remotely like this, please know you are not alone. It's not your fault, no matter what that voice in your head says. You don't have to carry it all by yourself. Please, let someone love you through it. I wish I had been able to do that for myself.

In closing to this chapter, I'll share a poem I wrote about 5 years ago. I'd like to dedicate it to all of you, men and women, who have suffered any form of assault or abuse. I wrote it with Mother Earth and the feminine in mind, but I think it captures the plight of anyone who has ever been assaulted or abused. May it bring to you whatever you need it to.

The Plight of the Feminine

Her heart is feeling broken.

Words of love always left unspoken.

Always feeling she is being used, for thousands of years, battered and abused.
Consistent attempts to banish her light, this has been her never-ending plight.

She's not really sure how much more she can take.

Consciously think about your choices and actions when another heart is at stake.
Her boundaries and limits have been pushed too far, day after day, scar after scar.

Listen up, because this is the deal, she'll do whatever is necessary,
at this point, to mend and to heal.

~Audra Rene Weeks

CHAPTER 12

He Came In the Dead of Night

Even the darkest night will end and the sun will rise.

~Victor Hugo
-Les Miserables-

At around 3 AM, he crept silently into the house. He quietly set a roll of duct tape and a knife on the stairs. He entered my room; as I peacefully slept, he stood over me. He lifted a 2X2 piece of wood and swung it at my head as hard as he could. The club shattered, throwing shards of wood across the entire room. He put his hands around my neck. He squeezed, harder and harder – he didn't stop – it was his intent to strangle me to death.

September 6, 1991 is a night that still haunts me.

⌒

After Amber was born, David and I struggled. We fought all the time. We had been great friends, but we weren't great as a couple. I was working so hard to remain responsible and be the adult and mother she deserved; David just wanted to smoke pot. He couldn't hold down a job, and we were living off of the generosity of his family and the state of Arizona. I knew this couldn't last, and had my eyes out for a new situation.

When Amber was about 14-months old, my Aunt T, who had been living in California, decided to leave her husband, Russ, and move back to Arizona. Aunt T, her two daughters, and two sons moved to Payson, a small town about two hours from New River. About a month after Aunt T left Russ, he followed her to Payson to be closer to his kids, the girls. Aunt T's boys had a different father.

Russ acclimated pretty quickly in Payson. He had been a lawyer in California, and became a substitute teacher, crisis counselor, and kids' coach in Payson. By all accounts, he was a pillar of the community.

Almost a year after my aunt's move, she made me an offer that would potentially help us both out. She asked me if I would live with her during the week and help her with her kids. In return, she would buy a decent car that I could use to go to college up there in Payson. I would go back to New River on weekends to see David and my mom. It seemed like a great opportunity; I could help Aunt T, and kickstart my own life. What could go wrong?

It ended up being way more than I, a naive, 20-year-old, new mom, bargained for. Aunt T was working long hours on a road crew and wasn't home much. My cousins were 2, 5, 10, and 14. Their care, especially that of the two youngest, Russ's girls, was primarily my responsibility. Of course. I also had the responsibility of caring for my own 14-month old daughter. I was in over my head.

Things began to unravel fairly quickly between my aunt and Russ soon after I arrived. My aunt was seeing someone else, and she and Russ started fighting about custody and visitation. At one point, I actually witnessed a physical altercation between the two of them.

I had liked Russ. I had always gotten along with him. But I was often put in the middle. Aunt T expected me to withhold any unauthorized visitation that Russ attempted if she was not home. Russ would show up when he wasn't supposed to be there, and I had to play bad cop, blocking Russ's access to his daughters. It was very stressful, and I started to resent my aunt for putting me in that situation. Of course, I was still an expert at swallowing my own feelings, so I never approached Aunt T about it. As a result, she had no idea of the tremendous pressure I was under.

I even began to have nightmares about Russ and the kids. On one of the weekends I went home, I confided in my mom, who was Aunt T's sister. I told her about a vivid dream I had recently had. In the dream, Russ was trying to kill me and his girls. I have no idea where anyone else was in the dream; it was just me, Russ, and the girls. Desperate to protect them, I hid them in the dryer. I told them to be quiet while I tried to fight Russ off.

The dream and its after-effects were frightening. Even once I woke, I was terrified. I had no idea why I had dreamt such a terrifying scenario.

My mom encouraged me to talk to Aunt T about how I was feeling. I was intimidated by Aunt T; there was no way I was going to open up to her. At the time, Aunt T had a very strong personality, and I was an insecure barely-adult. Perhaps I was projecting my insecurities, but I was sure that any such conversation would result in Aunt T dismissing my fears and telling me to stop acting like a baby. In fact, I begged my mom not to tell Aunt T about the dream.

I also told my mom that I did not want to go back to Payson. The situation was more than I could handle. With the long hours that Aunt T was working and her new relationship, I was being asked to do too much. She may not have realized it, but Aunt T was able to live her new life relatively unencumbered, while my life was non-stop child-care. I was overwhelmed; it was more than I should have been asked to do.

⌒

After the physical altercation between Aunt T and Russ, she had an order of protection put on him. He was no longer allowed to approach the house. When he did, I was the one tasked with turning him away. One night, after I had already had The Dream, I asked Aunt T to stay home instead of going to her boyfriend's house. I was afraid, and I didn't want to be the only adult in the house that night. I expressed my fears to her, but she didn't stay. That stuck with me.

I had been in Payson for about 5 weeks at this point. David had come up, on this particular day with a friend, to help him get his car out of impound. I was going back to New River within the next couple of days, so he took Amber home with him that evening.

Aunt T's oldest son had just moved to Texas to live with his dad and start his freshman year of high school. That night, I would stay in his room downstairs, instead of upstairs in Aunt T's room, where we had both been sleeping. Aunt T was home on this night. She managed the kids and I watched the MTV music awards on T.V. It was a nice break for me. I was looking forward to having a room and a bed to myself. I was tired and at peace when I finally went to sleep that night, shortly after 11:00.

Little did I know the terror that awaited me.

An explosion. A kaleidoscope of the universe − brilliant flashes of light and movement, like I was traveling through it. And then, darkness. Something was terribly wrong! I could feel the duress within my body that something wasn't right. I managed to open my eyes, and I found myself looking right at him. I was looking at Russ. It must have scared him to see me wake up because his eyes widened in what can only be described as panic. He must have thought he knocked me unconscious with that blow to my head, but instead he had woken me up.

As I became more aware, I realized that I could not breathe! Russ had begun choking me before I was fully conscious. When I opened my eyes and he saw me looking right at him, he began violently shaking me by the neck. His grip was so tight; I couldn't pull his hands from me. I was clawing at his hands, trying to get them off.

I was hearing what seemed to be a clicking noise echoing in my head. "Kkk... Kkkk... Kkkk!" It was so loud! How was no one else hearing this? Why was no one else woken by that ripping sound and rushing to help me?

I realized what the sound was: It was me. It was the sound I was making, trying desperately to get oxygen beyond just the back of my throat and into my lungs.

Although everything was happening in real-time and speed, it was all in slow motion to me. There must have been moonlight coming in through the windows, because although I could see shadows in the darkness, I was able to clearly make out everything in the room, including his face. Frozen in time, my eyes shifted around the room looking for someone to help me. I looked past Russ to the doorway of the bedroom waiting for my aunt to appear to rescue me... waiting for anyone to appear to help me. No one came. No one was coming.

It is insane the adrenaline that surges through your body when it comes down to life or death: fight or flight at its peak moment. I chose to fight. In that moment of sheer and utter terror, I chose to do everything in my power to live.

I was able to get one leg, my right one, in between myself and his upper body. I was in a full, one-legged, crunch position and I forced my leg to straighten, pushing him away from me. I swear, in that moment, my leg had bionic or supernatural powers. In reality, it was pure adrenaline and the leg strength I had from years of playing soccer.

I was strong enough to push hard enough to force this 6'1", 220 lb man off of me. He relinquished his grip, and with that last surge of energy I had, I screamed. Deafened by terror, I can only imagine what those blood-curdling screams must have sounded like to someone else. In that instant, he was forced to let go and run. My screams followed him as he turned and ran out the kitchen door and back into the night.

I was up and out of that bed in one fluid motion, making my way to the stairs. When I rounded the corner and looked up, they were all already standing there. My aunt, my 10-year-old cousin, and my 5-year-old cousin. The 2-year-old was blessedly still in her crib. Over and over and over I said, "Aunt T, Russ tried to kill me! He tried to kill me! Russ tried to kill me!" I was absolutely hysterical!

My aunt thought I had been dreaming. My mom had told her about my dream, despite my plea for her not to. When Aunt T saw the blood coming from my head, she assumed I had hit my head on the headboard of the bed, which made the dream seem more real to me, and the cause of the blood.

Still not convinced, she asked me where he went, and I told her, "Out the kitchen door!" I was pleading with her to call the police and she wouldn't, which made me even more hysterical. What the fuck was wrong with her!? Call the police! We need help! I need help!

Instead, she was going to go see for herself that I wasn't dreaming. I don't think she understood that I was mentally and emotionally still very much in that room alone fighting for my life, waiting for help that wouldn't come. The moment was over, but I was still living it. All I wanted was to know that someone was on their way, that help was coming, and she wouldn't make the call.

He Came In the Dead of Night   111

When she decided to leave me and the kids upstairs while she walked downstairs to verify my story, I thought I was going to lose my mind. Sanity was actually slipping away from the amount of terror I was experiencing. She calmly walked downstairs while I felt like I was still suffocating.

Finally, she saw what she needed to see – the kitchen door ajar – and came right back up and made the call.

I think it's important for me to stop here and attempt to explain the imprinting that happened within me at that moment. She chose not to make that call immediately, and any trust I had in her instantly dissipated. It may sound extreme and unjust. After all, she was acting from a more rational place. She thought I was dreaming and didn't see any urgency to act. She wanted to make sure before she made an emergency call. This sounds like a completely legitimate and rational decision. In all honesty, I may have made the same decision if the tables had been turned. But they weren't. I was having a completely different experience than she was.

My immediate needs for survival during the assault were oxygen and assistance. I received neither. My immediate needs after Russ fled was for medical and emotional assistance, and physical safety. These could not be met by children nor by Aunt T. She did not meet any of my immediate needs in my state of duress, so the imprint occurred. Any trust I had for her to meet my needs and protect me was lost. In the moment, I did not realize this was happening, but it absolutely was.

I had just experienced one of the deepest levels of trauma there is. There was absolutely nothing rational in what Russ did to me, and there was absolutely nothing rational in what I experienced during the actual event nor what I experienced in the minutes after. I was compiling imprints in that high emotional state that had resulted from intense trauma.

This phenomenon is very hard to put into words, but I believe it is what causes PTSD sufferers to experience their past traumas in the present. It's like a repeating echo. But instead of the echo getting ever-smaller on outward-bound sound waves, it's all trapped. Like a ball bouncing around inside a pinball machine, the brain has to repeatedly re-experience the physical and emotional stress caused by the trauma.

The Sheriff's Department finally arrived, along with a detective, and the manhunt was on. Payson is spread out in a wooded, rugged area. They brought in dogs to track him through the forest. Although there was a lot of chaos going on, for me it was welcomed. The chaos meant that someone was helping.

I sat on the couch as the kids sat across the room, staring at me, with horror on their faces. I think the 5-year-old might have actually been afraid of me. I'm sure I terrified her with my screams.

Maybe they were scared because of the extreme amount of terror they saw me display. Maybe it was the blood in my hair and on my clothes. I'm sure the magnitude of what they had witnessed from me and the sound of my screams was tremendous enough for them to have imprints of their own. Maybe they were just scared *for* me. Maybe they were just in total shock by all of it. I'm not sure, but they just sat there, staring at me.

The adrenaline that had been surging through my body, had kept me from feeling my injuries, but now I could feel it all. I had been bludgeoned on the left side of my head – the source of my kaleidoscopic experience. It was bruised, swollen, and relentlessly throbbing.

My neck was bruised and painful, and my esophagus and Adam's apple hurt every time I swallowed.

The detective asked me a few brief questions for his initial report. He began his investigation in the bedroom. When he asked me if I could positively identify Russ as the perpetrator, I said, "Yes, absolutely." I looked over at the kids as I said that because, ugh, that was their dad. The detective told me he would have more questions for me later, but wanted me to get checked out by the EMTs.

I just wanted my mom. Like, right that minute! I needed to hear her voice. I needed her to know what had happened to me. I needed to know that she was on her way to be with me. Aunt T had told me it was too early to call her. I don't even know if it was 4 AM yet, but still, REALLY!? My mother wouldn't want to be bothered about an attempt on my life until she had her morning coffee? I mean, you have got to be kidding me!

The EMTs said I needed to go to the hospital to be checked for possible concussion and skull fracture. I know the detective was concerned that I might need stitches. They were going to take me by ambulance but my aunt insisted on taking me herself. For the record, I didn't want her to take me. I can't remember if I expressed that out loud, but it's how I felt, for sure. I wanted to go by ambulance because that felt safer to me. All I wanted was to feel safe.

In the police report, the detective said that he bagged my clothes as evidence and took pictures of my injuries before I went to the hospital. Although I'm sure that happened, I don't remember it.

My aunt took the kids next door to the neighbor's house or a friend came over to stay with them so she could take me to the hospital. Another detail I can't quite remember. I think the ambulance escorted us and a Sheriff followed.

Honestly, the trip to and the actual visit to the hospital are a bit of a blur for me. I know I checked out physically fine and I didn't need stitches. I didn't have a concussion or a fracture. The hospital staff told me that I was lucky. I remember laughing with them and Aunt T about being hard-headed in more ways than one. I was also told that based on the bruising on my neck, I shouldn't have been able to scream. And I could still talk. Their comments made me feel strong like I was a walking miracle, rather than a victim.

Aunt T and I went back to the house, and at some point, my mom arrived. All the details seem to elude me. I was in a state of total shock; I was still very much struggling to find my way mentally and emotionally out of that bedroom. I do know that my mom's presence made all the difference in the world to me. There was so much going on, so much pain, anger, uncertainty, and fear. She was the calm in the storm for me. She was definitely the person I wanted most.

In their search for Russ, the Sheriff's Department dispatched a team to his house to look for anything that would help them find him. They found a list of scenarios wadded up in his trash can. It was a pro/con list of different scenarios he had been pondering. It was absolutely horrifying and disgusting! Some of the options were (paraphrasing): "take girls killing 4," "take girls without killing," and a few others. Perhaps most tellingly, the option to "kill everyone in the house except T, as revenge on her," was deemed the "easiest scenario of all". I believe his intent was to kill everyone except my aunt.

If his intent had been to just knock me out and bind me, he would have brought the duck tape into my room rather than putting it on the stairs to grab as he went up. He also wouldn't have tried to strangle me before he even knew I was awake unless his intent was to kill me. No, I definitely think his intentions were to kill multiple people in the house, including me, his own children, his stepson, and my 1-year-old baby, had she been there.

One of the first calls my aunt had made after calling the local Sheriff was to a detective in California. He arrived later in the day. Evidently, this detective had been investigating the murder of a woman who had been beaten to death in her sleep about three years earlier. She had been one of Russ's clients, and he said he considered her a friend.

Russ had been one of the first people allowed on scene of the murder because he was the lawyer handling the victim's estate. As time went by and the investigation continued, Russ became the primary suspect. The California detective had uncovered that Russ had embezzled money from her trust account, and he built the case from there. He was moving to charge Russ with murder, but Aunt T had provided an alibi. Without very strong evidence, and with an alibi from his wife, the case went cold.

I learned all of this after Russ had attempted to beat me to death. It became very clear: Russ was a murderer, and he had almost succeeded in murdering me and four young children. That my aunt would keep this from me, even when she knew I was uncomfortable with him, was a really hard pill for me to swallow.

She knew. She knew that he had been and still was a murder suspect. She had actually been questioned about it in the past. In fact, once their arrangement in Arizona became volatile, she contacted Santa Clara County Police Department in California to indicate that she had *lied about his alibi;* she could *not* vouch for his whereabouts on the night of the murder.

She shared additional information with the Payson and California investigators about Russ: he was obsessed with serial murderer Ted

Bundy; he had read a book about him over a dozen times. He believed in Bundy's idea that you could get away with murder if the victim were a perfect stranger, since there would be nothing to tie you to the crime.

These are things I would have liked to know.

Aunt T knew that I had been having nightmares and that I was scared; my mom had told her. But she never indicated that she knew Russ was a potentially dangerous person. She never gave me the chance to opt out of our agreement when things started getting volatile with her and Russ. I had even asked her to stay home one night, because I was scared, but she still left to see her boyfriend.

All of this was very difficult for me to understand and process, not only at the time, but over the years that followed.

For the record, I don't blame my aunt for what happened to me. Yes, there are several things that I was very angry, hurt, and resentful about, but in the end she was not the person in the room trying to kill me. She also has no control over the actions of someone else, only her own.

So now, we all knew, beyond a shadow of doubt. He had killed that woman, and he was still out there somewhere, perhaps nearby. I sat there terrified, trying to process how close I had come to death, that I had come face-to-face with a cold-hearted killer and fought him off. This man had violently and brutally beat a woman to death with a flashlight and a hammer.

And then came the survivor's guilt. Why had I lived to tell about my experience, while the other woman had not? She was dead. He murdered her over $5,376 that he had embezzled from her trust account.

Back at Aunt T's house after being discharged from the hospital, I just wanted to go home! I wanted to get the hell out of there, but as a material witness, I had to stay in case the detectives had more questions.

My dad, who had been living in Hawaii at the time, called. He was still a mostly absent father; I don't remember seeing him at all during his 5-year residency in Hawaii. My mom had put in an emergency call to him to let him know what had happened. At first, I was so grateful that he had called, that I could talk to someone who would empathize with what I had been through... what I was still going through. When I told him what had happened, his response shocked me. He sounded relieved! He had worried that it was his ex-girlfriend, a drug addict, that had reached me somehow and had been harassing me. He was relieved that he was blameless. That conversation crushed me.

I had been through so much during the years for which my dad wasn't there to protect me or support me. I don't know if he was even aware about what I had been through with my stepdad. I know he didn't know about the rape; no one did. I had been very nearly murdered, in a very brutal fashion, and that was his response!? Maybe he was in shock, or maybe he didn't know what he *could* say or how to handle it? I don't know, but his non-response validated every belief of abandonment that I had, and reinforced my feeling that he did not love me or care about me. I was certainly not a priority.

⌒

At some point, even though I was still scared to be alone, I mustered the courage to take a shower. I didn't feel good at all. I still had dried blood matted in my hair and the yucky residual energy of Russ and what he had done to me all over me. Although I wanted to wash myself clean of that lingering energy, I was not looking forward to the pain I would endure while washing my hair with that wound on my head.

When the evening approached, I felt myself slowly going into a panic. It would soon be dark, and everyone would be going to sleep. I was absolutely terrified. I lay in my aunt's bed and listened while my mom gave the girls a bath. I could hear my older cousin, the 5-year-old, explain to her 2-year-old sister that daddy was a "bad man". She explained to her that he had come in the night and hurt me. I listened as she told my mom, "Aunt Jacque, Audra's screams were scarier and louder than thunder!" For a 5-year-old to come up with that analogy is beyond me. My heart broke to hear how scary that was for her, and for the fact that she was living in a new reality with regard to her father. I lay there and listened, feeling completely powerless, guilty over the terror I had caused all three of the kids with my screaming.

An off-duty officer had offered to come and stay the night at the house with us. I was a basket case awaiting his arrival. I was so tired. I was mentally, physically, and emotionally tapped out. I was in so much fear of the night that I straight-up felt like a lunatic.

I don't think anyone in the house had any understanding at all of what I was going through. How could they possibly understand? There was nothing they could say to make me feel better, absolutely nothing. Comments like, "calm down" or "everything is going to be okay" left me wanting to scream in frustration. They were completely ignorant of what I had been through and what I was still going through. These condescending comments were actually insulting and felt demeaning. I wanted to shout, "Trade places with me, and let's see how you feel. You were not in the room with me as I literally fought for my life in absolute terror. Don't tell me to 'calm down'!"

Were these things being said in an attempt to actually bring comfort to me? Or were they saying it for their own comfort? Was I expected to keep my fear and behavior around it in check to benefit myself, or to placate those around me? I think the more appropriate things to say would have been, "What can we do to help you? What do you need? Do you want to talk about it? Is there anything we can do to make this easier for you?"

I'm so sorry my discomfort makes you uncomfortable. Here, let me "calm down" and pretend that nothing happened and that I'm fine so you can feel better.

⌇

When the off-duty officer got there, I felt a tremendous sense of relief. It's interesting how a stranger brought that for me and my own family couldn't. He slept on the couch, in the living room, and I slept on the floor, right next to the couch. My sleep was restless to say the least, but I did find some rest. It would be years before I would ever sleep peacefully again.

The next day seemed much more low-key as far as the investigation went. My aunt and I had answered the barrage of questions the detectives had the day before. Although the Sheriff's Department was still on a manhunt for Russ, they had gotten pretty much all the information they needed from me, so they were going to let me go home.

My aunt made calls around to hotels and such for a safe place for her and the kids to go. I left alone, close to dusk, to make the hour and a half journey home. I will NEVER forget that drive home! There are a lot of hills coming out of Strawberry going into Camp Verde. Every time I would descend a hill, the headlights from the cars behind me would disappear. Each time, I thought it was Russ, popping up from the back seat with his head blocking the rear-view mirror, blocking the lights behind me. Even though I logically knew he wasn't in the car, I could not stop this physical reaction from happening. I would feel a rush of heat followed by a wave of absolute terror move through my entire body. This happened EVERY. SINGLE. TIME I went over a hill. It was debilitating, and there were points during the drive that I didn't think I could mentally, physically, or emotionally make it home. It was an absolutely frightening drive!

As I drove, I held on to the thought that once I made it home, far away from the scene of the crime, and I got to see my daughter and David, that all my fear would disappear.

Not at all the case.

It was dark when I arrived, which brought with it all the same fears from the night prior.

Shortly after I arrived home, my mom called. She told me that the Sheriff's had Russ in custody. This was at first a relief, but then she told me the details: While the manhunt was on, he had made his way back to my aunt's house and hid in a treehouse in her backyard. He had been up there, all that day, listening to us inside the house. After everyone had left, he broke into the house.

When my aunt and the kids arrived at the hotel, she realized she had left the paper with the list of hotels she had called at the house. She realized Russ could use this information to find them, so she called the Sheriff's Department and asked them to go to the house and retrieve that paper. When they arrived, they saw that the house had already been broken into. They searched the house and found Russ inside, hiding in a large cupboard in one of the upstairs bedrooms, clutching a kitchen knife. He was so tightly crammed in the cupboard that they had to physically pry him out of it.

You would think that I would have rested much better that night knowing they had caught him. I did not. I was still absolutely terrified to go to sleep. Catching him solved nothing for me. I asked David to stay awake and keep watch so I could sleep. I woke up sometime in the night hysterical because he had fallen asleep. I was inconsolable. I was inconsolable every night after the sun went down for months.

⁓

Russ accepted a plea agreement. In exchange for a videotaped confession of the brutal murder of his client in California, the death penalty was taken off the table. His charges in Arizona were also reduced from Attempt to Commit First Degree Murder to Aggravated Assault with a Deadly Weapon or dangerous instrument.

I had mixed feelings about the plea agreement. After becoming aware of Russ's murderous tendencies, and knowing that I narrowly escaped death in that bedroom, along with the aftermath of continued terror, to have the court say that he had only "assaulted" me was tough. I understand why it was done though. We all wanted to ensure that he would receive maximum sentencing with no chance of a 'not guilty' finding. The plea was a sure thing. It also spared us the trauma of a possible long and drawn-out trial.

The sentencing hearing was a tough day, indeed. It was the first time I had seen Russ since the night he tried to kill me. Being in the same room with him felt like I was suffocating all over again. My aunt, my mom, and I had all written letters to the court. We were given the opportunity to read them aloud and to speak to the court.

My aunt was a champ, and her letter was very powerful and well-written. When it was my turn, I stood up and tried to speak. I was paralyzed with fear being in the same room with Russ. Instead of speaking, I made weeping sounds, trying to fight back my terror and my tears. It was like his hands were wrapped around my neck all over again. I gasped and choked, and was unable to speak coherently.

Seeing my distress, and knowing that I, as the victim, should be given every opportunity to have my thoughts on the record, the judge allowed me a moment to gather myself and try again.

There was so much I wanted to say to the judge. I wanted to tell him about the constant state of terror I lived in since that night. I wanted to tell him that every night, as soon as the sun went down, I turned into a basket case. I couldn't sleep; I had nightmares all the time, even when I was awake. I wanted to tell him that I struggled to mother my own baby, and that I cried all the time. My constant state of terror was destroying my life. It was destroying me from the inside, and there was nothing anybody around me could do to help me or make it better. I was trapped in a living nightmare from which I couldn't wake.

When I went to speak the second time, the same thing happened. I just stood there and looked at the judge and wept. He allowed me to step out of the courtroom with the District Attorney. The DA and I decided that he would speak on my behalf. We returned to the courtroom, and the DA read my statement for the record.

I think my honest attempt to say something and my inability to do so spoke volumes that day. Russ was sentenced to 18 years for the crimes he committed in Arizona. Russ was extradited to California for sentencing after everything came to a close in Arizona.

Although I was not in attendance at these proceedings, I did provide a written statement. This is what that judge had to say, "My concluding comments for the record to Ms. Weeks, I thank you very much for your comments. The activities of the defendant in Arizona and in other relationships outside the one that is covered principally by this report are very illuminating because it does, I think, clearly bring home to the court and to anyone who reads this report, notwithstanding the defendant's background or education or whatever his position was in the community, he is truly one of the most dangerous psycho-paths I have ever seen. And I say that based upon my eighteen and a half years on the bench. And I will keep my comments very short based upon that.

I would caution the department of corrections in Arizona or in California and personally state that I have grave reservations that this defendant will ever be sufficiently rehabilitated that he should be con-sidered for parole. Or to say it another way, I think there is a strong likelihood this defendant needs to remain in prison for the balance of his life."

Russ was sentenced to life in prison by the state of Califor-nia, to be served concurrently with his Arizona sentence. A life sentence is truly not a life sentence; he came up for parole twice before he died of natural causes in prison. This meant that I had to go through two parole hearings over the years before it was finally over.

A few months after the sentencing was over, the television show "A Current Affair" aired the story of Russ. I watched, as I'm sure mil-lions of others did, a reenactment of that night in that bedroom. It was very surreal to watch it on T.V., as a spectator. It made me sick to my stomach to watch a stranger playing my part in something that was very real and so personal. It was just a script to them, while I still suffered tremendously from the reality of it all. Clips were shown of his videotaped confession of the murder of the woman in California. I watched as he laughed in those clips, after giving gruesome details of that murder, like it was nothing. Truly psychotic.

There was talk of a possible T.V. movie being made about the full story, but it never happened. Russ is now a case study though. He's classified as a sociopath. If you take a psychology class, you may learn about him alongside other sociopaths like Ted Bundy.

⌒

A movie about Ted Bundy recently came out on Netflix. As I watched, it made me realize that, although no one will ever really understand what I went through, I will also never know what it was like for my aunt or my cousins.

This is actually a very profound awareness for me. It took any residual judgment I had left out of the situation for me. It helped me see, with much more clarity and with much more compassion, that I wasn't the only victim. We were all victims, in one form or another. Even family members and friends who weren't even there were affected and survived it, too. Each of us had a completely different experience based on what happened, what parts we played, where we were in life, what emotional tools and resources we had to cope, and filters that were already within us from our past experiences.

Since I am a master at repressing emotions as a coping mechanism, that is of course what I did. But there were some things I could not escape. I could not escape the intense fear that made its presence known every night as the sun went down. I could not escape the nightmares when I closed my eyes. I could not escape the daytime heat rushes of fear that went through my body. I could not escape the terrifying flashbacks that occurred when a loud noise triggered them or when I saw a man who resembled Russ.

To try to get past this debilitating anxiety and fear, I went to counseling a few times. I was looking for instant relief, and that was not something the counselor could provide. She tried to tell me that I had to take a journey that I was just not ready to take. She wanted me to talk about not only my feelings about what happened in that bedroom that night, but also every event and my emotional responses throughout my entire life. Are you kidding me? Sorry lady, but that's not how we do it around here. Cue: imaginary carpet and broom, please.

CHAPTER 13

PTSD

Your soul stained my shoulders.
My whole life smells like you.
This will take time.
Undoing you from my blood.

~Nayyirah Waheed
-The Work-

According to the American Psychiatric Association, Post Traumatic Stress Disorder (PTSD) can occur in people who have experienced or witnessed a traumatic event. Women are twice as likely as men to have PTSD. There are 4 main symptom categories of PTSD, which can vary in frequency and severity.

Intrusive thoughts such as repeated, involuntary memories; distressing dreams; or flashbacks of the traumatic event. Flashbacks may be so vivid that people feel they are re-living the traumatic experience or seeing it before their eyes.

Avoiding reminders of the traumatic event may include avoiding people, places, activities, objects, and situations that bring on distressing memories. People may try to avoid remembering or thinking about the traumatic event. They may resist talking about what happened or how they feel about it.

Negative thoughts and feelings may include ongoing and distorted beliefs about oneself or others; ongoing fear, horror, anger, guilt or shame; much less interest in activities previously enjoyed; or feeling detached or estranged from others.

Arousal and reactive symptoms may include being irritable and having angry outbursts; behaving recklessly or in a self-destructive way; being easily startled; or having problems concentrating or sleeping.

Many people who are exposed to a traumatic event experience symptoms like those described above in the days following the event. But for a person to be diagnosed with PTSD, symptoms last for more than a month. Symptoms often persist for months and sometimes years. For people with PTSD, the symptoms cause significant distress or problems functioning. PTSD often occurs with or exacerbates other related conditions, such as depression, substance use, memory problems, and other physical and mental health problems.

⁓

I definitely have experienced PTSD. My self-destructive behavior started almost immediately after my first experience with my stepdad and got much worse after the second experience. I absolutely see it, with clarity, after I was raped. But where I see it in the most extreme is after the attempted murder. I experienced PTSD for years after that.

In order to be diagnosed with PTSD, you must exhibit at least one symptom in every category. I no longer have any symptoms in category 1, intrusive thoughts. I still have some symptoms around all my traumatic experiences. However, how the traumas show up in my life today is called traumatic response, not PTSD. The difference is that with PTSD not only do you have symptoms in all 4 categories, PTSD is a collection of distorted or exaggerated responses to triggers around the traumatic events, while "traumatic response" is some of these distorted responses when triggered, but on a much more reasonable and manageable level.

⌒

Although the effects around my childhood and young adult relationship with my dad did not cause PTSD, I definitely experienced some pretty extreme triggers and traumatic response. I had created many detrimental mistaken beliefs and core beliefs about myself from that relationship.

To this day, I have obstacles around abandonment and self-worth. A perceived sign of possible abandonment in any relationship can trigger irrational thoughts and behavior for me. It's much more extreme in my relationships with men. Dating can be very challenging for me. I am triggered often, and I have to be very mindful of my thoughts around what's true and what's not.

It got so bad that I used to toss away who I really was in an attempt to secure a relationship. I put on a significant number of masks and changed my behavior in order to feel worthy of being loved and accepted. I worked to become exactly what I thought someone else wanted me to be in desperation, especially with men. Many times, I completely threw my true self away in hopes that they wouldn't abandon me. My goodness, I've come a long way from all of this.

⌒

Regarding my brother's suicide, I don't think what I experienced was PTSD. I did however experience traumatic response. The event itself, as well as the way my family dealt with it, created unhealthy beliefs around grief. It was very traumatic to witness what my mother and the entire family went through. Not to mention the devastating changes I witnessed in my brother before he committed suicide. The result was that, since the age of 8, I have tried to hide and cover up any feelings of grief and sadness. The pressure of not dealing with these emotions bled through though to the rest of my life. It presented itself as manic behavior as a child, and substance abuse as I got older. My psyche did what it needed to do to cover the pain up and numb it down. I pretended.

I had a difficult time confiding in my mom about the big things, and there were a lot of big things! I was terrified to rock her boat in any way after what she went through regarding Mark's death. Rather than disrupt her, I went into emotional seclusion. This rippled into other relationships. I've shouldered a lot on my own out of fear that people wouldn't be able to handle all the things I've done, what I've been through, or my feelings around all of it. If a discussion was going to make someone else feel uncomfortable, I remained silent instead. I've gotten much better at this, however, I am still a work in progress. I still have a tendency to seclude myself and work through problems on my own rather than reach out.

⌒

I experienced PTSD for well over a year after my stepdad's verbalization of his desire to molest me. Just his expression of his thoughts felt like an emotional molestation. Having to live with him after this event, I had very intrusive thoughts and was in fear most of the time. I became self-destructive, to say the least. The intrusive thoughts did not subside until I moved in with my friend Tammy. But the traumatic responses continued and amplified about a year later when he attempted to assault me.

One of the results was that, well into adulthood, I had paranoid thoughts that older men wanted to molest me. Not all older men;

just the ones who complimented my looks or my hair. I still have a hard time receiving compliments from men who are older than me. I don't fear they will molest me anymore, but a compliment can still be a trigger, and it can make me feel as vulnerable as I did as a child.

I experience traumatic response as a result of my stepdad's actions even more than 30 years later. I created some detrimental core beliefs that I'm still deconstructing, and I still get triggered as a result.

After I was raped, I experienced PTSD for months. I had intrusive thoughts and nightmares quite often. I withdrew from my life and became a bit reclusive compared to my natural state and personality. Although I made better choices, it was more out of fear of what might happen rather than a desire for personal improvement. As a result of the rape, I experienced true depression for the first time, along with a tremendous amount of negative feelings around my self-worth. This experience, the rape, validated every core belief that I had that I was worthless. I felt so ashamed to be me. I thought that if anyone found out, I would be forever unlovable. It also made me more fearful of men. Now it wasn't just older men who wanted to violate me sexually, it was any man.

Even now, I feel shame as the result of being a rape victim. I'm still triggered often. The act of dating brings with it so many individual triggers of which I have become intensely aware. I think part of the reason these feelings are so deeply entrenched has to do with how long I kept the rape secret and carried the burden alone. I also think I am still in some denial, which allows me to feel artificially free for a while until a trigger is hit, launching me into traumatic response all over again.

It is probably not surprising that I experienced PTSD most deeply and enduringly after Russ attempted to murder me. I suffered from full-blown PTSD for roughly 7 years after this event. It then subsided to the less severe traumatic response, but at each parole hearing, I was thrown into another months-long bout of PTSD.

This meant that I experienced flashbacks during waking state and nightmares at night. I started using drugs again to help me stay awake, even though I had been clean for over two years. I felt the need to stay awake because I was terrified that, if I fell asleep, someone would try to kill me. And then I needed to use drugs to escape my reality, which I could not handle. Ultimately, I again fell into a pattern of self-destructive drug abuse for years. I finally cleaned up again when I became pregnant with my son, Dylan.

But after he was born, I completely went off the deep end for almost two more years. It's hard for me to admit, but it was so bad that I'm surprised I survived. My kids, Amber and Dylan, saved my life; without them, I think I might have killed myself. My will to die definitely outweighed my will to live, but my children trumped everything. Because of them, I am happy to say that I cleaned up again right before Dylan turned 2, and I never looked back. That was 23 years ago.

For years after the attempted murder, I would lie awake at night and play out scenarios in my mind. What if someone came through this door or this window? How would I escape and save my kids too? Scenario after scenario would run through my mind until I felt I had a solid game plan for each one. If sleeping arrangements changed from one night to the next – one of the kids was gone or I was sleeping somewhere else – I would have to run through the scenarios all over again. It was exhausting. This nightly ritual did not stop until I got together with my now ex-husband, which was six years after the actual event.

My kids learned how they could wake me up to minimize the risk of me yelling. The best way was for them to just cry in their rooms until I heard them and went to them. Of course, this wasn't always the case. Sometimes they would have to come into our room when they were sick in the night or had bad dreams. They would stand right by my side of the bed and touch me to wake me up. I mean, no big deal right?

Sounds like what any kid would do. But the fear I experienced when being woken up like that presented as straight-up rage. That gentle touch scared the shit out of me! In turn, I unintentionally scared them with my behavior and anger. How awful for them to not feel emotionally safe to wake me up when they needed me. My kids were genuinely afraid to wake me up.

They had to be in bad shape or really scared before they would try to wake me. Dylan had periodic nightmares and learned to just bring his pillow and blanket into our room and go to sleep on our floor, without having been comforted, rather than wake me up. This makes me feel sick inside as a mom.

They learned that they had to stand three or four feet away from the bed or at the doorway of my room and just say, "Mom." It still startled me, and I would react with irritation, but it was much better than if they touched me.

At the time, none of us understood why I responded this way. We all just thought I hated being woken up, like I was just mean and selfish about sleep. None of us realized it was a traumatic response. I talked to my counselor about this because I didn't understand where the anger and rage came from. She explained that when triggered, the brain cannot disassociate from the event being triggered; your brain actually thinks you are experiencing the event. You go into fight or flight mode, and rage is a very common attribute in fight mode.

I still have traumatic responses around this. Certain sounds trigger me and I will get a heat rush through my body and I will feel brief anger. I think it might have something to do with whatever sounds my subconscious mind heard when that wood hit my head while I was sleeping. I seem to be more triggered when the sound is high-pitched. I also have a hard time managing practical jokes when it entails someone jumping out and scaring me. I have to warn my friends about this.

I have much more awareness around my triggers now, which helps tremendously in verbalizing my limits. I can even ride out some very triggering moments once I see them for what they are.

PTSD and traumatic responses are very real phenomena, and they can show up in many different ways for many different reasons. If you know someone who suffers from PTSD or traumatic response, try not to take the behavior or responses personally. Speaking from experience, I can tell you that something that seems like harmless fun to you can launch a PTSD sufferer into a terrified emotional state. You have no idea what someone else may be going through or what they have gone through. Before you judge, remember that they may have endured terrifying experiences that have left them struggling to slay their demons. Let's try to be kind to one another.

CHAPTER 14

THE HEALING WORK
PART 2

I caught sight of my reflection.
I caught in the window.
I saw the darkness in my heart.
I saw the signs of my undoing.
They had been there from the start.
And the darkness still has work to do.
The knotted cords untying.
The Heated and the Holy,
oh they're sitting there on high
so secure with everything they're buying.

"Blood of Eden"

~Peter Gabriel

ssignment two, writing out all of my traumas, was definitely tough. Although I hadn't written them out in significant detail, like I did for this book, it was enough for me to begin to acknowledge what had happened to me, and realize there had been significant, long-term, damage done. It was the first time I saw, in black and white, the ridiculously long string of events that had left me so traumatized. It was devastating. How was I still alive? Looking at the written paragraphs, I couldn't believe that all of these things had happened to me, and I had lived through them.

That list of summaries started to crack the veneer that I had so securely placed over all of my suppressed emotions. But it was too much. I was not prepared for the onslaught of emotion that was coming at me. It took my breath away, suffocated me. It was too intense.

As I began this journey, the intensity of the uncorked emotions often left me wanting to curl up in a fetal position. They were paralyzing. I wanted to stop. There were times when I thought it would be easier to just die rather than to walk through this horrifying terrorscape. How was I going to survive this?

⌒

When I was little, I was a ray of sunshine. I remember teachers using this exact phrase to describe me. They also said I was a shining star, full of life, full of love, free-spirited, caring, encouraging to those around me, and other uplifting phrases. At the time, I knew this about myself; I could see and feel this within myself. From a very young age, I could see that I was able to make those around me feel very happy and loved. I had a talent for bringing comfort and a smile to anyone who was hurting or suffering. I drew them in so I could touch them with love. My light was insanely bright and those around me saw it, felt it, and remarked on it.

⌒

As the traumas began unfolding in my life and taking their tolls on me, I couldn't imagine what I had possibly done to merit any of them. I think I believed that it was this very light that kept attracting these monsters – like a beacon. Like moths to the flame, they couldn't help themselves. They were drawn in, stealing my essence little by little. The continuous stream of darkness kept coming, devouring my light.

⌒

There is always a driving factor when we make self-destructive and harmful choices. I take full accountability for each and every choice I've made, but something drove me there. Healthy choices are the privilege of healthy people. Destructive choices are made by people who have been wounded.

When I read the chapters I have written, I can see that I made destructive choice after destructive choice. I can see when they started. Against all logic, I seemed to be doing my best to extinguish my own light. I wonder if there was something within me that believed that if I extinguished my own light, maybe the monsters would stop coming; maybe they wouldn't see me anymore.

⌒

These chapters around the traumas were excruciating for me to write. In writing them, I relived each and every one. It was a tremendous undertaking to remember and relive the traumas, but it was almost harder for me to acknowledge what I was doing to myself; it was actually heartbreaking.

Part of assignment two was reading out loud to Mireya what I had written for my homework. She listened intently to every word for the core beliefs that I had created within my subconscious mind.

As I read, she began creating a list of the beliefs that emerged from my words. As we discussed what I had written, she continued to listen, and she continued adding to that list.

This is how I met the Puppet Master.

CHAPTER 15

MEETING THE PUPPET MASTER

It's not really letting go of the past that is the problem. It is coming to terms with letting go of a possible future that will never be. That is the struggle. The mind wants to keep its fantasies. Even when they are wrong, unhealthy, dangerous, or even cruel. To let go of the past you must let go of the future and live in the present.

~Unknown

*U*pon completion of the reading and discussion of my traumas, Mireya brought to my attention a sheet at the back of my Week Two homework packet. In bold words across the top it said, "Stuck Point Log". Below that, were empty lines for me to list my own stuck points/core beliefs.

Mireya began listing the stuck points she had noted as she listened to me. She began saying them out loud so I could hear them. One by one, I wrote them down on my log.

This was such a powerful exercise. Remembering this moment has my tears flowing once again. I will never EVER forget how devastated and how heartbroken I felt. Even though each stuck point made absolute sense to me, I was shocked when I heard all of the negative things that I had believed about myself and others for almost my entire life. How could someone with such a loving heart and beautiful spirit believe these things about herself? No wonder I was in so much pain! No wonder I felt so alone!

Although a few were added as I continued therapy, this is the culminated list of the stuck points – the core beliefs I had about myself that were stopping me from being healthy:

- We don't show our pain or grief.
- People I love, especially males, will abandon me.
- I am not lovable, or I am hard to love.
- I am not worth investing in.
- I am not first priority.
- My feelings don't matter.
- I don't matter.
- I am not worth choosing.
- I am not safe when I am vulnerable.
- People close to me will hurt me.
- We just forgot about my brother.
- I was promiscuous, so it was my fault.
- Men will take advantage of me.
- I need to be loved
- I have to be perfect.
- I am broken.
- I am alone.
- I need something outside of myself to fill me up.
- I feel like I need to have control.
- I am not a good sister because I can't remember.
- I believe my aunt took advantage of me. It's her fault.
- My dad didn't love me.

- It was my fault neither of my dads knew how to love me.
- There's something wrong with me.
- I am not enough.

As I transcribed this list, I cried, A LOT! Having been a student and a current practitioner in hypnotherapy, I was very aware of how the subconscious mind works. The realization that my subconscious had been running a program geared around most of these beliefs since I was a small child, genuinely devastated me. I felt like my entire life had been stolen from me.

To understand how important the subconscious mind is in your life, I like this analogy: Your subconscious mind is like a computer. The Program is updated throughout your life, but from birth to age 7 is the most critical time. The Program created during this time will be the baseline program your subconscious will run; everything else will be built upon this foundation for the duration of your life unless you are able to reprogram it.

Your subconscious collects data based on your interpretations about your experiences and stores it as fact. Information received from your parents, other family members, teachers, or anyone else of influence gets stored away. Your subconscious doesn't have feelings or an opinion, so everything is stored, even if it's nothing more than an opinion – your own or someone else's.

The programming created from this outside information is where one's own strong beliefs around religion, politics, racism, sexism, etc. come from. If you ever examine why you believe so strongly about something, you might find that, it's not really even your belief. Rather, it was a belief given to you by outside influences. It was given to you through *their* filters and the Program *they* were running. You just think it's yours because it's all you've ever known. Even other people's fears and phobias can be projected onto you.

Not only has a lot of your baseline program been built on outside influences, but also through your interpretations of the life around you when you were a small child. A child isn't terribly good at logic or discernment when interpreting something. A child that cannot understand yet, that her emotions don't necessarily represent objective truth. Yet, as a child, your subconscious created the core beliefs through which you now make most of your choices.

⌒

There was always so much beautiful life happening around me, and I missed a lot of it. My subconscious was very busy focusing my conscious mind on the things that validated these negative beliefs. The subconscious mind filters everything around you and tells your conscious mind what is important, what to notice, and what to validate based on this baseline program. Therefore, my reality was seeing and experiencing myself as a negative; positive experiences couldn't be validated by the Program, so they were thrown out.

The grief I endured as we worked through my programming was off the charts. I had no control over my tears for weeks. I also felt very angry. I felt completely cheated out of my own life. I realized that I had lived my entire life as a puppet on strings. The Puppet Master was this Program created by a traumatized child. The Program had been infiltrated by fear-based thoughts and beliefs – a computer virus, if you will. I struggled tremendously to let this piece of awareness go so I could move forward. Sometimes I still feel angry about it, and I find myself grieving the what could have beens.

Although I was devastated, I was also grateful. Through this experience, I was able to cut the strings and become my own master. So many people will never have this awareness. You can't fix or change something if you are absolutely oblivious to its existence, so many people will go through life being unnecessarily miserable. They will go through life using core beliefs that are completely outdated, and were possibly never true to begin with. They will continue to live as the puppet.

Even in the midst of that soul-baring exercise, I had gratitude. I was grateful because I knew that, no matter how devastating it was for me to see the filters I had been experiencing life through, I now had the power to literally change how I would experience life from that moment forward. I would no longer be the puppet.

In my opinion, this was a true Awakening. If you are lucky enough to go through this experience, it will awaken in you the awareness that your Program... which you had very little conscious part in creating... has been dictating everything you do. It's just the pattern; it's literally why history keeps repeating itself in our lives and even in the world.

The Awakening is having awareness of our Program. The Awakening is the dismantling, the shattering, of this Program, changing our paradigm of life experiences. The Awakening is where we get the opportunity to see beyond the veil of what we were told to see, and who we were told to be. It gives us the chance to see who we really are in our core, in our soul.

Awakening to the existence of our Program gives us the chance to take our sovereignty back and to finally become the true physical manifestations of the creator of all things that we are. From here we can create our life based on what we truly see and feel the truth is in our own hearts, disregarding the Program. Awakening gives us the opportunity to create in love rather than in fear. The Awakening gives us the opportunity to stop the negative cycles and patterns in their tracks. Imagine what the world would look like if we all Awakened.

Audra Weeks
October 24, 2017 ·

Healing journey update:
I'm getting ready for my 7th session as I write this. Week 1 and 2 were brutal! My homework was to write out all traumas with as much detail as possible, and in doing this, the list of core beliefs became evident. It was a very painful and exhausting process with a lot of uncontrollable tears but it was worth it.
I finally had a voice and I felt heard. I also had an understand in where the healing need to, and can take place. Before I was just in a lot of denial knowing I needed to heal, but was afraid to face it all.
Week 3 and 4 was realizing through my homework exercises some of the things that trigger the core beliefs, and I could see them in action.
A lot of anger and resentment during these weeks. Angry at the things that happened and also all the moments it's all been stealing and affecting everyday after, for years!
Week 5 and 6 the homework has been challenging the core beliefs and challenging thoughts about the events themselves. It's been pretty intense and very eye opening.
I've felt a lot physical pain which I attribute to an outward manifestation of what's going on inside of me. So much to release.
I've felt a lot of disgust in these weeks. I've also noticed myself in behaviors I'm trying to drop. Unfortunately, it's a comfort zone because it's what I'm used to. When things that are important to me fall through or I'm stressed or excessively tired, I find myself replaying the broken record. I'm grateful for such awareness. I will continue to show up and do the best I can no matter what that looks like.
Thank you all for sharing this journey with me and for all the love and support I receive. So much gratitude for all of you. I love you!
PEACE and LOVE

 65   49 Comments

CHAPTER 16

THE SHATTERING

In order for the new to arrive, we must first allow the old to shatter. Sometimes this happens on its own. And sometimes it requires that we do the smashing. To tear apart what we've built because things have changed, including you. To admit that while it once was aligned, now it no longer is. This shattering requires both courage and faith. Courage to let go and faith that the pieces will come back together again in a way that is more aligned than it was before.

"Rise Sister Rise"

~Rebecca Campbell

Once I had my Awakening, I began doing the work to shatter the Program. I accepted the challenge to come completely undone. This meant questioning and challenging every single one of those core beliefs. This was my unraveling.

Mireya gave me packets weekly with worksheets that helped me get to the truth that resided underneath all the lies. One by one, I tore the beliefs apart and began the process of wiping them out. I will give you a couple of examples of my actual work so you can see what this looks like. It's pretty amazing!

⌒

I worked on identifying "Patterns of Problematic Thinking".

Q: = Question and A: = My answer

Bold Text = Core Belief/Stuck Point that I'm addressing.

Q: What beliefs do you have that cause you to jump to conclusions when the evidence is lacking or even contradictory?

A: **My feelings don't matter:** Even though I know that people care, my core belief pushes me to think that when my needs are not being met, it is because people don't care about my feelings, or that it is some sort of personal attack.

Q: What beliefs do you have that cause you to exaggerate or minimize a situation (blow things out of proportion or shrink their importance inappropriately)?

A: **People I love, especially males, will abandon me**: The word "abandon" seems pretty exaggerated. The truth is, people are meant to come in and out of our lives. The truth is, my dad did not leave my life and never come back.

I am not lovable or I am hard to love: The truth is, just because my dad didn't know how I needed to be loved or how to meet my needs, it's not a reflection of me or how hard or easy it is to love me.

We just forgot my brother: The truth is, no one forgot him.

Q: What beliefs do you have that cause you to disregard important aspects of a situation?

A: **My dad didn't love me:** The aspect that I've disregarded is that my dad did the best he could. He worked out of town, but he was always kind and loving toward me when we did spend time together.

I am not a first priority: The aspect that I've disregarded is that my dad did his best. He lived out of town a lot. He really did not know how to prioritize me or any of the family. He had not been a first priority to his parents either.

It's my aunt's fault because she took advantage of me: The aspect that I've disregarded is that she had no control over other people's actions.

I was promiscuous so it was my fault: The aspect that I've disregarded is that no one ever has the right to touch me unless I give consent, no matter the circumstances.

Q: What beliefs do you have that cause you to oversimplify things as good/bad or right/wrong?

A: **I have to be perfect:** Thinking that anything but perfect is bad or wrong.

I am alone: Thinking there is something bad or wrong with being single, that being single is the same as being alone.

Q: What beliefs do you have that cause you to Over-generalize from a single incident (a negative event is seen as a never-ending pattern)?

A: **We never show our pain or grief.** The truth is, everyone did the best they could with my brother's death. The depth of the grief and our inability to handle its outward expression made it feel easier to not discuss it.

Men will always take advantage of me: I have developed a fear that this is just how men are. The truth is, a few bad experiences doesn't dictate all men in my entire life.

People close to me will hurt me. This has happened to me on several occasions, and I fear it will keep happening. The truth is, I have tons of people who are close to me who haven't hurt me.

Q: What beliefs do you have that cause you to perform emotional reasoning (you have a feeling and assume there must be a reason)?

A: **I need something outside myself to fill me up.** I have feelings of emptiness, so I assume that I am empty or else I wouldn't feel this way.

I feel like I need to have control. If I have control, I can manage or control my emotions or can get what I need.

I am broken. People keep hurting me more than my fare share. Why?

I am not enough. Why am I single? I must not be enough for anyone.

I don't matter. Bad things keep happening to me. People keep leaving me and hurting me. I must not matter.

The next step was to challenge my core beliefs/stuck points. Although I did a worksheet on every single one of my core beliefs, I think one example will give you a good glimpse of what this looks like.

Column A

Situation: Describe the event leading to the unpleasant feeling.

A: My step dad's desire and attempt to molest me. A peer/friend raped me. A relative tried to kill me. My dad was not a participating parent.

Column B

Thought/Stuck Point/Core Belief: Write thought/stuck point related to column A.

A: People close to me will hurt me.

Column C

Challenging Thoughts: Use Challenging Questions to examine your automatic thought from column B. Determine if the thought is balanced and factual or if it is extreme.

Q: Evidence for? A: I had several experiences that validated this belief.

Q: Evidence against? A: I've had so many experiences to the contrary.

Q: Habit or fact? A: Both. The fact is that I have had several experiences that validate this. However, I had created a habit of thinking it was going to always happen and continue to happen.

Q: Interpretations not accurate? A: Only on my dad's account

Q: Extreme or exaggerated? A: Exaggerated in that I thought it was always going to happen.

Q: Source reliable? A: Yes and no. I am aware that some of this belief had come from when I was a child. A child is not a reliable source.

Q: Based on feelings or facts? A: Both

Column D

Identify the Problematic Patterns

A: The problematic pattern is, Over-generalizing: Thinking something is more likely to happen because it has happened in the past...

Column E

What can you say instead of the stuck point you've identified in column B? How else can you interpret the event instead of using that stuck point?

A: Instead of saying, "People close to me will hurt me," I can say, "A small percentage of people close to me have hurt me. That doesn't mean everyone close to me will."

⁓

For weeks I completed worksheet after worksheet, challenging each of these beliefs. Most of these beliefs were created when I was a child; as an adult, I could see that most of them were actually mistaken beliefs. A child doesn't have a whole lot of logic or reason, so they make up a story to help them make sense of things. This results in a lot of mistaken beliefs that the subconscious mind stores as a fact. I was able to see this very clearly as I worked through the worksheets. It was clear that most of these core beliefs were created through the eyes of a little girl who didn't know any better. She didn't understand the grown-up parts in any of it, especially when it came to why her dad wasn't there.

Not all core beliefs are created from the ages of 0-7. These are just the most impactful years as the foundation is being laid. Also, when trauma happens in your life, there is a tremendous amount of emotional stress, and therefore a lot of irrational thinking; emotionally, you become childlike. Intense traumatic experiences literally leave imprints on your subconscious mind, your physical body, and your energetic body.

One of the most satisfying things about doing the work was being able to see the truth. I was able to see how the beliefs came about in the first place. It made it easier to forgive myself because in essence, I was forgiving a child. At the end of each worksheet, I was able to restate the belief based on more truthful information. I was able to replace the belief that had been hurting me with one that would actually serve me.

Although the shattering was a very painful process, things started really changing within me for the better. I now had awareness almost instantly when I was being triggered into emotional responses based on the old Program; I was then able to reroute my thoughts in a more positive direction. I started experiencing life differently. My self-esteem and self-worth began to grow, and with that came a greater love for myself. This painful work was definitely worth it! I escaped my prison of the mind, and I found my freedom. I was no longer the puppet.

At the end of week 7, I said goodbye to AFG. I came to realize that I had stayed connected with him all this time because he validated a lot of my core beliefs. Once I saw more clearly, I realized that continuing a relationship with him could actually set me back. Unconsciously, that relationship could throw me back into beliefs like I wasn't enough or that I wasn't worth choosing, the relationship was no longer appropriate.

I let him go and he let me go too. Although we both cried, it wasn't as hard as I thought it was going to be. I did have a meltdown in that first week, but it had to do with so much more than just him. I was letting go of a part of myself, and I was grieving that. Letting him go was very symbolic, but it was also a physical manifestation of how far I'd come. I was letting go of the part of myself where all those beliefs had resided.

In the past, we had never gone longer than 6 months without one of us reaching out to the other. Upon this writing, it has been 1 year and 3 months since I said goodbye to him. Although I will always have a love for him, this was the right decision.

Audra Weeks
November 26, 2017 • Phoenix • 👥   •••

Healing journey update:
It's going pretty good!
I only have a couple sessions left, believe it or not! Wow, it's gone by sooooo fast!
I've learned a tremendous amount about my self. I've seen a more truthful perspective about some of my feelings that were pretty intense, and I've also seen where I probably should have had much stronger feelings than I did.
It's been amazing to me how the process has worked, and how I've literally been able to see the foundations come apart on core beliefs in my life.
This week, my homework was/is challenging beliefs around self esteem. I've done 3 and have 3 more. I'm procrastinating as I'm give you all this update. LOL.
Last week was 4 on power and control. Next week, my last week, it will be on intimacy. There will be 5 I'll be challenging on that topic.
I've been really seeing a lot of the collateral beauty these traumas and the healing journey have brought to my life. I believe that I have reached a point in my life, because of the healing that needed to take place, and the courage to take the journey that so many people will never reach.
I have learned so much. I have grown so much, in so many ways. I have an awareness that, I too believe, many will never have, and it continues to grow. I have a lot to be grateful for through all of this.
I'm still working through some feelings around how long it took me to get to the awareness of needing healing, and also what I put myself through to bring that awareness into the light. I believe in the timing of things and who know, maybe I was paying back some karma.
One of the most profound things that I have become aware of is this, I absolutely love who I am. I absolutely love how I think, how I process, how I feel, how I learn, how I love. I love the desire I have to evolve. I have had more than my fair share of ridiculously traumatic events in my life, and I could have turned out to a be completely different person because of them.
To be honest, I could have turned out to be a total asshole person with some pretty legitimate reasons why. I could have let the event extinguish my light, my joy, my passion, my desire to love my fellow humans. Instead, in spite of these events, I chose to be the loving, caring,
compassionate, passionate, humorous, bright light that I AM. I AM so incredibly grateful for my strength.
I've been doing a lot more meditating, and I have been observing my thoughts more rather than participating. I get to choose which thoughts I'm going to invest in, which is something else I've learned, and have been really mindful of.
Thank you for sharing in this journey with me. The support I have received has really helped me tremendously, and the messages I've received, on how sharing publicly has helped so many other people, has given me the courage to continue to share publicly. 🤍🤍🤍
PEACE and LOVE

 Audra Weeks and 40 others   28 Comments

CHAPTER 17

THE HEALING WORK
PART 3

Only when we're brave enough to explore the darkness will we discover the infinite power of our light.

~Brene Brown

*E*ven though I had finished the 12 weeks of cognitive therapy, I still recognized that getting past a lifetime of significant trauma was going to require more work. I knew that I wasn't magically healed after only 12 weeks of processing and homework. I knew that I would have to continue to be mindful and take each day as it came. I knew that there would still be bumps in the road ahead.

But I have made a tremendous amount of progress. To make that progress, I have made many significant changes in my mindset. Even though I still have some pretty tough days, I have so much more awareness; I have the mental tools to help me get through them much more efficiently. No more being the puppet. I am now the master.

Audra Weeks
December 8, 2017 · 👥   ···

Healing journey update:
Tuesday is my last day of the 12 week cognitive processing.
This last week was challenging core beliefs around intimacy. It was tough,
But not as tough as a lot of the other weeks. I've definitely noticed how the
intensity has been turned waaaaay down on my emotions. Thoughts pass
very quickly. I am about 90% less likely to engage in old patterned thinking,
feeling and behavior. It's pretty incredible. I am still working on genuinely
stepping into the rewrites. (Core beliefs rewritten that will serve my life in a
much more healthy and loving way. They are much more aligned with who I
truly am.
I am releasing a lot of abandonment and self worth issues still. I've noticed
I've had a lot more compulsive eating these last few weeks. Thank goodness
I work out or my body image issues would be through the roof! LOL....
I have taken responsibility for my part in how I have allowed myself to be
treated in my male relationships. I've allowed behavior and treatment that I
would have never allowed in my female relationships. Right now, I'm seeing
a zero tolerance on my part regarding males, and I'm trying to find a balance
without burning the house down. No more one sided friendships, and if the
behavior and actions show validation of the old core beliefs, I'm out. Bye
Bye. I'm going to continue going to counseling. I'm going every 2 weeks now
instead of every week. I've got some homework from last week that I'm
working on for the next session. I'm rewriting the impact statement on the 5
traumas plus one that came out a few weeks ago, that happened a few years
ago, that I allowed to go on way to long!
I look forward to every day, gently releasing the old and implementing the
new. It's a totally different experience that feels much better, and again,
more aligned with who I AM.
This journey has proven to be well worth the discomfort and the work! I'm
looking forward to continued growth and my becoming.
Thank you everyone who has been following, supporting, and loving me
through this! 🩶
PEACE and LOVE

 57   23 Comments

CHAPTER 18

THE SHIFT

The Law of Detachment

In detachment lies the wisdom of uncertainty...in the wisdom of uncertainty lies the freedom from our past, from the known, which is the prison of past conditioning.

And in our willingness to step into the unknown, the field of all possibilities, we surrender ourselves to the creative mind that orchestrates the dance of the universe.

~Deepak Chopra

'd like to take this opportunity to come full circle and show where some of my growth has been and how far I've come. I'd like to show you some of the fruits of my labor! I started this book out by sharing two very painful dating experiences that perfectly exposed and validated the deeply seated core beliefs I had. These experiences showed me my unhealed wounds; they were the catalysts for the beginning of my Hero's Journey.

Shortly after I finished the 12 weeks of cognitive therapy, I rejoined a dating website. I know! Here we are again! Through therapy, continued life experiences, and really evaluating my life, I had come to fully realize that we really do attract our experiences. We call them in for specific reasons so that we can learn and grow in whatever ways we need to. So, I now understood that it hadn't been the dating site experience that was awful; it was that my psyche had needed to show me my wounds. Dating the men who did that for me was painful, but that was ultimately what I needed at the time.

Now that I had done so much soul-searching and had begun to heal, I needed to see what was different. I wanted to see the changes I had made put into action. At this point, I hadn't dated for about a year and a half. After my last physical encounter with PTG, I had taken myself out of the dating field. Prior to therapy, besides being at my wits' end, I felt that it was important for me to take the time to work on and sit with myself without distraction. Don't get me wrong, I went on a few dates with interested friends, but I was only interested in platonic relationships.

I had several successful dates through the website, and I noticed that my approach and behavior during the dates was much different than before therapy. Did I flounder around a little? Well, of course I did! Dating is kind of scary for the most well-adjusted among us. I was dealing with the added burden of processing and integrating my new core beliefs. It takes a while to rewrite and put into practice a new way of being. I have found that this new template is constantly evolving as I continue to grow, learn, and heal.

Part of me still needed a relationship, but I was no longer willing to settle for less than what I knew I deserved and wanted to experience. If I didn't feel he was emotionally going to be able to complement my life and grow with me, even if I felt attracted to him, I let him go.

I was no longer trying to shoehorn someone into my life just for the sake of having someone. I was no longer willing to take in a fixer-upper hoping that he would magically become the man I wanted. I accepted who they showed me they were. I no longer tolerated men who were only looking for sex. I paid attention to the red flags. My new template made dating a very empowering experience. I met some good men, just not the right one for me.

I have to admit that I did feel some frustration. I had grown enough to see that I was now attracting a different type of man. My problem was that I finally felt ready to have a significant other in my life, and it still wasn't happening. I knew I had a lot to bring to the table, yet I couldn't quash the lingering mind chatter that there was still something broken within me. Rather than feed into that old Program, I just continued moving forward on my journey. I believe in Divine timing, and I knew in my heart that it would happen at the right time with the right man; I leaned into that.

For the next 3 months, I was very pleased with the many changes I saw within myself even though I was still walking away single.

I did begin building a friendship with one man. Although he lives in a different state, we 'matched' while he was in Phoenix for a work conference. I want to share what my growth looked like through this experience. This dating site experience was totally different from the others; my continued experience with him is where I really saw, felt, and put into practice 'The Shift'.

His name is Adam. He is 36 and has never been married. It seems he's single most of the time. I really liked his take on relationships – or maybe it was *my* take on his thoughts around relationships; maybe both. I am going to try and relay all of this the best I can with it being my perception of Adam and maybe not necessarily his perception of himself.

Adam has been in some long-term relationships, but tends to get bored or need space. Is it possible he has commitment issues or a fear of fully engaging to avoid feeling loss? Maybe. Or maybe he's comfortable with himself and doesn't need to be in a relationship to feel whole. Maybe, it's a mixture of all of this.

I had been single for around 7 years and had been really getting comfortable with myself for 2 years. I had grown to value my long stretches of time alone, so I can understand the need for space. But if both people don't have the same need for space, this can pose a problem. One person's need for space can exacerbate the insecurities of the other. A person with less need for space might think there is something wrong with the relationship if their partner wanted some alone time. Although Adam may need more space than I do, after all my own growth and solitude, I understand that need and do not see it as a threat to the relationship.

Adam seemed to really understand this about himself, and didn't stay in relationships with people who could not handle it. Or maybe he just hasn't met the woman who sets his soul on fire, someone with whom he *wants* to spend more of his time. Whatever the reason, the fact that Adam is brave enough to eschew Society's idea that "singlehood" is to be avoided is an attractive quality, in my opinion. Adam has already mastered the self-assuredness that I have been working on for the past several years.

⌒

When I look back at my pre-journey experiences, I can clearly see when a relationship wasn't working anymore; it had run its course, yet I stayed in it. There are a variety of reasons we stay in broken relationships. We stay because it's what we are taught to do even when it's no longer good for us. We might also stay "for the kids", when in fact a bad relationship is often more damaging to them than a breakup. Finances can keep us in a relationship. We might stay because it's easier to stick with a known quantity than to take a paralyzing risk with the unknown. We might stay simply because we fear being alone.

Seeing my past dating experiences with great clarity, I now wanted to pursue an intimate relationship with non-attachment.

⌒

An intimate relationship with non-attachment is a relationship in which both parties agree that physical intimacy is not the defining factor. Those involved work together to define the relationship's rules and boundaries.

Does that mean being in a relationship that lacks commitment and loyalty? If that is the agreement, then, yes. Is this arrangement one in which the partners do not give 100%? Such a relationship probably wouldn't stand the test of time, but it is up to those involved to decide. Will there be obstacles? As with any relationship, yes. Partners may have trouble staying true to the agreement without wanting to move it in another direction.

A relationship of non-attachment does not lack connection. In fact, the partners must be very in-tune to each other's needs in order to agree to the stipulations they set up. If the relationship is going to last, communication is absolutely required. The partners have to continually gage and reassess their own and their partner's needs, even modifying the arrangement as necessary. Often, the relationship develops into a "traditional", long term relationship. But if the communication breaks down, or one party's needs are no longer being met, the relationship naturally dissolves with no complications.

Attachment is an action and it is fear-based. You are not making choices based on your needs; instead, you become dependent on someone else for your happiness. That dependency ultimately causes you to suffer, because there is no way someone else can satisfy everything for you. And since you fear change, you attach to what's there, even when it is not what you need. Letting go of what is no longer working is a struggle, and causes more fear. Your fear traps you in a broken relationship, and all hope for real happiness is dashed. This is true for all aspects of life, not just intimate relationships.

What a relationship of non-attachment lacks is *forced* connection. To me, this means letting your partner be who they are, without trying to change them. Do not tie them down with fear.

"The beginning of love is to let those we love be perfectly themselves, and not to twist them to fit our own image. Otherwise, we love only the reflection of ourselves we find in them." (Thomas Merton: No Man Is An Island)

In my case, I am ultimately looking for a long term relationship, but only if we both feel the same way. Neither should feel trapped.

People should have the opportunity to be who they are, only making changes when they want to for themselves, not because someone else needs them to. If who they are, what they want, or where they are in life doesn't work for you, then let them go. You will both find someone better suited for your experience. I promise!

$$\sim$$

I had been considering pursuing an intimate relationship of non-attachment long before I started talking to Adam, but his approach to relationships seemed to embody the idea. He seemed to get it right and was actually living it, changing no one, and releasing the relationship when it was no longer working.

We exchanged messages quite frequently when we first connected. It was new and we were getting to know each other on a basic level. There was flirting and a desire to meet in person, but I lived in

Phoenix, and he lived in Texas. So we both just moved forward with our individual lives as we continued our friendship, regardless of the distance and with no desperation to meet. The fact that he lived out of state made it much easier for me to put the non-attachment piece into practice. It was easy to let things be as they were without needing them to be anything else.

⁓

As Adam and I got to know each other better, our conversations got a lot more intimate and sexual in nature. We didn't talk on the phone very often but when we did, the conversations were generally long ones. I felt safe to be expressive in ways that I hadn't been in a very long time. It was fun, and I felt really comfortable with him. He always talked to me with respect and integrity, no matter what we were talking about. He never used language that would trigger my old, negative core beliefs. He was definitely mirroring back to me something new. That in itself was very refreshing for me. I credit the self-work I had done along with who he is as a person for having such a good experience.

⁓

Adam is smart and seems to be more left-brained; he definitely seems to run more on logic than emotion. I'm not sure how he is at work, but in social situations, he doesn't seem to overthink things. He just rolls with what is happening and seems to let life move him along. That being said, although it seems he lets life move him freely, he doesn't really seem to be moved by life. It sounds weird and doesn't make much sense, does it? This may make more sense. If you asked him what sets his soul on fire, his answer would probably sound like, "I don't know." Does that make more sense? This may make it sound like he doesn't enjoy himself or have fun in life or that he isn't a passionate person, but that really is the farthest thing from the truth. Maybe it's me observing that he flows in the middle where I tend to experience things a little more intensely or on the extreme sides.

Adam's emotional maturity manifests itself in compassion and empathy. Even without a background of traumatic experiences, he seems to understand that my traumas have altered my approach to life and all of its stress. He is patient and he listens. He's just a natural.

About four months after Adam and I started talking, I decided I was going to write this book. I know he likes to read a good book and he's fairly well-read, so I decided to share a couple of chapters with him. He's the first male I shared my book with. He is such a source of emotional safety to me, that I had the courage to share some very intense and vulnerable material with him. I wanted to get his opinion as a reader and as a man. I offered him the chapters on AFG, PTG, and my breaking point.

Shortly after I handed off those chapters of my most vulnerable self, my anxiety went through the roof! Although I had similar reactions after sharing my pages with my closest girlfriends, this was more intense since Adam was the first man to read any part of my book.

⌒

At this point in our friendship, we didn't message each other as much as we had in the beginning. Sometimes two or three weeks would go by before one of us would check in with the other; we'd catch up and then continue our own lives. So not hearing from him after I gave him the chapters was really nothing out of the ordinary. But, my insecurities had me making up stories: "He clearly does not want to talk to me anymore after reading about what I had been through." When I wrote those chapters, I still had a lot of humiliation, grief, and shame I was working through. Writing those chapters took me to a level of emotional rawness that I had never gotten to in therapy. I was so vulnerable that I can't even put into words the anxiety I felt, and here I had just shared those events with a man. I felt tremendously insecure and maybe even a little paranoid. I thought he must be feeling differently about me because of what he had just read. All the feelings of being unlovable because of the things I've been through were pounding on my door.

When I had a moment of clarity amidst all the nonsense, I decided to trust who he had always shown me he was, and I talked to him about it. The act of reaching out to him was an extremely vulnerable yet bold moment for me. I opened up with some babble that clearly showed my insecurities. I even told him that I was making up all kinds of stories around it before I found the courage to frame the actual question: did he feel differently about me because of what he had just read about me in my pages? I trusted him, but I was still terrified of what his response would be or worse yet, that there would be no response at all. He did reply, of course. He said "I can with 100% confidence say that I don't view you any differently since reading your pages. Promise." He didn't treat me differently or act like he now thought I was weird, crazy, fragile, or insecure. He didn't get uncomfortable or shut down like a lot of men would when he saw that I was going through a dramatic episode. He responded like a solid friend would, with no judgment.

Adam gave me some good advice and actually made some edits. It was his idea to write my chapter one the way I did. He felt identifying every trauma would be a gripping way to start the book and also aid in grabbing the male audience. He told me that the trauma I had endured and how I was able to survive it was so compelling that it didn't need anything else said to support it. I obviously thought it was a great idea, hence, 'My Mountains'.

One of the things I've been intrigued about with Adam is that his Program is not at all based on negative beliefs. Granted, he doesn't have a past full of trauma that would cause these core beliefs to emerge and play themselves out, but it has been incredibly interesting for me to observe someone that doesn't really get triggered. He's human, so I'm sure he does have triggers, but whatever they are, his response seems to be very subtle. I've come a long way in my reprogramming, but I still have my moments, and I still have work to do. Adam doesn't make my moments about him; he sees that they are about *my* responses to *my* perceived triggers. I think he is this way with everyone, not just me. Observing him, seeing how he reacts in different situations, gives me hope and courage to continue dismantling my negative core beliefs. I, too, do not want to keep anything around me that serves me poorly.

CHAPTER 19

THE MEET

When we think of "meant to be" we automatically assume forever.
But maybe it isn't supposed to last forever.

Maybe it's just someone who is in your life to teach
you something. Maybe the forever is not the person,
but what we gain from them.

~Unknown

I recently had a family event that was taking me to Texas. My niece was having a baby! This was her second baby, but there is a pretty big age gap between them; she almost felt like a first-time mom. My sister, her mom, had passed away about 10 years previously, so I knew that would be a big piece that she would be missing. Going there to help, if only for a few days, gave me the chance to not only be there for my niece but also for my sister. It was something I knew my sister would have wanted to be a part of if she were still here. It was a big deal to me. I was truly blessed to be able to support my niece and her family and to honor my sister.

I had planned my trip months in advance. I connected with Adam to see if it was a possibility to meet while I was there. Texas is huge, and I wasn't sure if I was going to be anywhere near him. It was, as they say, "meant to be", and it all worked out perfectly. After helping my niece and her family with the baby for about five days, they took me on the 45-minute drive to Adam's. I spent my last night and day with him; we actually got to spend his 36th birthday together!

The energy building up before 'The Meet' was intense for me. Adam and I had been talking for about 10 months at this point. Some of our conversations had included sex and various sexual fantasies. I hadn't been intimate with a man for over two years, and I really wanted the physical connection to be there when we actually met in person. If there wasn't going to be that instant attraction though, I knew that our night would be fun no matter what because of our emotional connection and the friendship we had built.

I'm delighted to say that the attraction was there. Without going into tremendous detail, and keeping this a family establishment, we had a lot of fun together! I learned a lot in that short amount of time spent with him. He showed me how a man should treat a woman in more ways than one. He gave me the opportunity to see where I have room to grow, and gently showed me where I can love myself more. Our experience together and our friendship in its entirety significantly raised the bar for my future relationships.

I did walk into the experience with some vulnerabilities as a woman. As I said, I hadn't opened myself up physically to a man in over 2 years. What if I forgot how to do this? You know, the typical ridiculous things we tell ourselves. I was also in the wrap-up stages of one of the heaviest menstrual cycles of my life, which incidentally started two weeks early and pretty much the minute I landed in Texas. Yes, I know, the irony! That was a really comfortable and fun conversation to open up the evening with, let me tell you!

I also was a little insecure about our age difference. Actually, not the age difference so much as the fact that I had had babies and quite frankly, having them was hard on my body. He's 11 years younger than I am, and he'd never had kids. I had no idea if he'd been with women who had been scarred by childbirth. Would he turn away? Even though his words and actions made me feel nothing other than sexy and beautiful, I had a nagging worry that he was thinking otherwise.

I have actually never had anyone have issues with my scars. That insecurity was completely internally developed. Adam's acceptance of my body made me realize that I have room for growth in this aspect of self-love.

In retrospect, I feel like I held back in many aspects with him. That's something that bothers me a little but not too much. It was, of course, the first time I had spent time with him. But, I had been working on always fully showing up no matter what. I didn't hold back on purpose or out of fear; I think I just felt a little dazed, like a deer in headlights. This isn't as heavy as it may sound; I am actually chuckling right now. I am fully aware that I am an extremely passionate woman. It had been so long since I had been with someone, the anticipation, the stimulation… everything hit me all at once, and it was overwhelming. But, it was definitely overwhelming in a very good way! I completely trusted Adam, but it was just a lot for me to take in. He may not have even noticed.

I'm not just talking in the physical sense either. I actually struggled a little in conversation too, which is not like me at all. It's almost as though I was sheltered when I could self-edit before pressing 'Send'. I was definitely more witty via text. I'm saying this through my own laughter but I think I was kind of in shock! I mean, it had been more than 2 years, and I found myself at a loss for words.

⌒

Needless to say, that was a fantastic night and day. But in the days and weeks to follow, I went through a minor mental and emotional crisis.

It bothered me that I couldn't just feel happy and peaceful about the fun experience I had just had.

I'm pretty sure that Adam dropped me off at the airport with feelings of contentment, and then just moved forward in life... zero disturbance. Not the case for me! Where was my non-attachment? Upon talking with close friends and Mireya, my counselor, about what I was going through, I concluded that this was pretty normal for a woman, especially one who had just had her first physically intimate experience in over two years. More than one of my confidants told me, "You wouldn't be human if you didn't have any feelings around it at all."

On our way back to his place after we had spent the day out for his birthday, Adam and I talked about our sexual experience. He was aware how long it had been for me before we ever met in person. I remember telling him, "It's like I can feel my body again." A very passionate part of myself that had been numb and asleep had awakened. This was challenging for me; the lioness was awake from hibernation, and she was hungry!

I honestly did not know what to do with this new appetite upon coming home. I had been flying high from endorphins, and the landing was not a smooth one. I had just been turned on, and I wanted more. That created a lot of confusion within me, to even recognize the hunger. It took me a minute to get my bearings and decipher what was really going on.

What was going on was this: my experience with Adam was very meaningful. He showed me what sex between caring partners could be like, and what a respect-based relationship should be. He opened my eyes to a vast array of possibilities within myself; I now saw growth paths that were hidden before. Since it was Adam who had helped me see all of this positivity, I wanted to attach to him. My training kicked in. I started putting things in perspective instead of letting my heightened emotions run the show. I sifted through my feelings to expose how I really felt about Adam. I realized that I was suffering from nothing more than residual euphoria and sexual energy. That sense of euphoria can be tricky! It can make you think that you are "in love".

This was a really good opportunity for me to see just how quickly attachment can happen and why. It also gave me the chance to step back and see it for what it really was. I was able to actively put non-attachment into practice for the first time. I allowed myself some time to let my newly-awakened body cool its jets. I recognized that I had just had a great experience with a phenomenal person. There was absolutely nothing wrong with wanting more of that in my life. From a place of non-attachment, I allowed myself to appreciate my time with Adam. I was able to let the fear that it might not ever happen again, pass.

That fear triggered the old programming based on old core beliefs to kick in. With it came a whole slew of fear-based feelings. For the first time since I began my therapy and self-work, I had experienced intense physical intimacy and euphoria, followed by a familiar fear. My subconscious was reverting to dealing with this fear using the old Program. It was nothing personal; it was just my subconscious mind doing its thing.

I think it's important for me to share this, even though it feels vulnerable for me to do so. It's important to show that completing therapy doesn't mean that everything is miraculously different. It's not all rainbows and unicorns. Dismantling the old ways takes time, awareness, and practice. It also takes experiences that give us the opportunity to say "No" to the old ways and "Yes" to the new that we are trying to create. It is a continuous process, but it gets easier.

The mind is extremely powerful, and it is very easy to buy into what it's telling us, even if what it's saying is not real at all. My mind told me, and I believed, that I was never going to meet another great guy to whom I was attracted. I believed that I wasn't enough because I didn't seem to be the woman that set Adam's soul on fire. I feared that having sex with Adam was going to change our friendship, that once he "got what he wanted", he would lose interest in me as a friend. My mind was trying to get me to run the old Program! Now I actually find these thoughts to be insulting to me and to Adam. I'm sorry Adam!

I am very grateful that I have the awareness I do now. That awareness is the key to escaping the prison of the mind and its old Program. I was able to see all of that nonsense for what it really was. I then was able to make a mindful choice rather than succumb to the puppet master. I wasn't having it; I was no longer a prisoner to the past conditioning of my mind. I took a step back from what was trying to happen and instead leaned into my new truths; I knew who Adam was as a person.

Yes, for a few weeks after meeting with Adam, things got a little messy for me. But, you know what? That's okay! It was an opportunity to use my awareness to make it through it fairly gracefully. I came out the other side with only minor bumps and bruises, and in the process, I learned a lot! I built a much better understanding of how and why attachment can happen, and how damaging it can be. I successfully responded to something that triggered that old Program. I'm walking away from the experience with an even greater awareness than I had before. And if I ever experience that again, I have confidence that I will be able to maneuver through it much more quickly and with more ease.

This is what rewiring the brain looks like.

⌒

Regarding Adam, I have no idea what the future holds for either of us, and I am completely okay with that unknown. What I do know is that, if the opportunity ever presents itself, I would love to spend more time with him. But either way, I am content and at peace. No matter what happens, nothing can ever change how I've experienced our friend-ship thus far. Thank you non-attachment.

I have a tremendous amount of gratitude for him. This man has given me the opportunity to learn so much throughout our friendship! He has given me so many gifts. In so many ways, he has helped me raise the bar for future relationships, and nothing can change that. It's already happened! He has given me much to take with me on my continued journey, and I hope that I have given him something to take on his.

In the spirit of non-attachment and a future of unknowns, I would like to share a poem with you that I wrote about 5 years ago. It truly is something that I try to be mindful about and try to put into practice in all aspects of my life. May it bring to you whatever you need it to.

THE CURRENT

I AM drifting within the current.

It is peaceful, it is kind, it is ALL loving.

It envelops me gently as it carries me to each point in and out of time.
It embraces me as we flow through every moment of my destiny.

I have no desire or need to worry that I will lack anything.
For within the current is everything.

It cradles me and rocks me and sings to me it's sweet lullaby.
As if I were its precious child.

I have no fear as to where the current carries me.

For to forsake me, would be to forsake itself.

Within the current I AM unconditional. I AM loved.

I AM safe.

I AM free.

For I AM the current, and the current is me.

~Audra Rene Weeks

CHAPTER 20

THE FINAL TREK

It takes a powerful person to cry out despite those who'd prefer the
convenience of silence. It takes a fearless person to allow their sadness
to come out from the tight box of cultural expectations to be expressed
and processed. And it takes a world of strength for that same person
to be true to their feelings, own their emotional territory - to walk into
the very chaos of its outright messiness - and uncover the paragons of
victory and joy that were held by them, for such an
aching long time, so quietly within.

~Susan Frybort

*W*riting this book was, by far, the hardest thing I have ever
done. Going through cognitive therapy was intense
and difficult, and writing about it took that intensity
and difficulty to a whole new level. I never could have imagined how
deep this journey, from catalyst to publication, was going to take me. I
can not begin to tell you the number of days I would have rather just
died than to continue on.

I had done so much work acknowledging, releasing, and healing in
therapy. I had walked through a tremendous amount of denial, fear,
sadness, anger, resentment, blame, humiliation, and most all, grief
and shame. I didn't know it then, but in therapy, I had really only

scratched the surface. It didn't occur to me that there was such an extensive amount of releasing and healing that still needed to take place. I had no idea what I would encounter, the darkness that I would have to walk through, to write this book. The book – writing process, which I refer to as "the dark night of the soul," was another Hero's Journey in itself. I can vividly remember when I first started writing, how terrified and vulnerable I felt. I could see my fear as I spilled it out in words. As I have gone back, reread, edited, and rewritten virtually every sentence dozens of times, I feel I have conquered that vulnerability. I read each chapter countless times before I could move on to the next. I would sit with many of the chapters for weeks before I was able to move forward. As I began to heal and expand, I went back again and again to reread and make alterations.

When I wrote chapters 3 and 4, "The House of Mirrors" and "Breaking Point", I experienced a tremendous amount of grief, guilt, and shame. It was debilitating. I self-isolated and cried a lot. I remember taking my computer with me pretty much everywhere I went. I had it not because I was writing wherever I was, but because I was terrified to leave the book unattended. I was pouring everything within me out onto the pages. I was baring my heart, soul, and perceived sins. The thought of leaving all of that on my desk or in a drawer was unimaginable to me. It was my constant companion.

Although I explored those two relationships during cognitive therapy, I still hadn't worked through all the shame and grief around them. As I was writing, I was ripping off the bandages on these old wounds and releasing a lot. The shame was so much that I often found it hard to leave my apartment. My life responsibilities and obligations were the only things that kept me in the land of the living. It really sucked writing those two chapters! It was heartbreaking to look back and see how poorly I allowed myself to be treated, what I tolerated, and just how small my sense of self-worth was.

The chapters about my dad and being raped were the hardest ones to write. The possibility of hurting my dad by shining the light on our early relationship was a very huge obstacle to overcome. Expressing how deeply his absence affected me, identifying the low self-worth and abandonment issues I still struggle with, and knowing he would likely read it was brutal. It was brutal because I know the damage that was done wasn't intentional on his part. But it had to be included, because it is the truth of what I experienced.

Even though being raped was one of the traumas I worked on in cognitive therapy, I realized I had only acknowledged that it had happened to me. I was still in a lot of denial around how it made me feel.

I was forced to sit with some extremely intense emotions when I started writing the chapter about it. As I dug into that event, I could not believe the wounds I uncovered. Paralyzing shame, anger, grief, denial, and sadness overwhelmed me. It was actually shocking to me how much emotional collateral damage I had been carrying.

This was the chapter that I could not read out loud to Mireya. I still cannot. Even though I continued to move forward, I went into a state of depression, just like I had after the rape. After a few months of trying to cope on my own, and after much thought and consideration, I asked my doctor to help. It was that bad. He prescribed a low-dose antidepressant, which I stayed on for about four months. I just recently went off of it; we'll see how it goes.

Along with the chapters about my dad and the rape, writing about my substance abuse as a recurring theme was challenging. I was tempted to just conveniently leave it out because I was so ashamed of it. How honest would that have been though? Leaving it out also would have meant leaving out the possibility of helping someone else who also had this burden. Healing and helping others is my whole point. Cue: big girl panties. I wanted to skip over the drugs and alcohol to avoid being judged by how I coped with my past. I am extremely proud of myself for pushing through that shame and exposing that part of my life. I remind myself that judgment is a reflection of the person judging, not of the person being judged. We all know this right?

The fear of judgment is so powerful; it's almost its own trauma. Writing about my drug and alcohol dependencies and seeing that narrative through has helped me release the shame around it. Seeing my whole story unfold and processing through it with my counselor brought so much clarity. It has helped me see that many of the choices I made that made me feel ashamed, weak, like a shitty person, small, or like a loser were deeper than they seemed. In reality, these choices were coping responses to trauma, core beliefs playing themselves out, and the influence of my siblings and their drug use that I saw growing up.

The "Healing Work" chapters were little lights in my writing journey. They reminded me of what I had already conquered, how far I had already come, and how much I had already grown. They were much-needed reminders whenever I felt like the darkness was going to swallow me up. They were somewhat clinical as well, giving me a break from dealing with the intensity of the core work.

Speaking of lights in my writing journey, "The Shift" and "The Meet" were extremely satisfying to work through. Those two chapters were fun to write! That content made me feel vulnerable, but I was also able to recount so much joy. The beauty in these two chapters filled me up and gave me what I needed to write the more difficult chapters.

⁓

I jumped a lot between chapters as I wrote; I could only handle so much at a time. I moved around and wrote what I could handle.

⁓

I dealt with some intense anger and grief when I wrote, "He Came in the Dead of Night" and "PTSD". I encountered feelings I had not allowed myself to feel when the actual event occurred and in the years that followed. As I wrote, I became infuriated at how much this event fucked up years of my life. I raged at how much one psychotic man's horrifying act stole from me.

Writing "PTSD" was an in-my-face, eyes-wide-open experience. Although neither of these chapters was pleasant to write, I acknowledged and released a lot of buried, pent-up emotion. Strangely, I actually felt guilty for being mad. As though I didn't have a right to be angry that there was an attempt on my life. I felt guilty that my anger might cause discomfort to someone else. Somehow I let myself off the hook and allowed myself to be angry anyway. I refuse to hide my feelings anymore; there's nothing wrong with me for having emotions. I own them, and I get to deal with them how I see fit.

⁓

I found that working out a lot over the course of therapy and writing helped me tremendously! Moving my body keeps everything else moving and flowing as well. Exercise is another form of expression and is also a great way to release the negative energy around emotions like frustration, anger, and grief.

In fact, I would like to give a huge shout out to Jabz, Boxing For Women, at Glendale Palms! I am grateful for the amazing trainers, workouts, and all the beautiful friendships I've made. Jabz, thank you for being my life preserver and for holding space for me to get through the unimaginable.

I took a lot of baths to help soothe my aching body and soul. I had a lot of inner pain that manifested itself physically. The baths were wonderfully healing and very metaphoric to the inner cleansing that was occurring.

I spent a lot of time alone. I listened to a lot of music. I allowed myself to cry in paralyzing pain and grief that I didn't think I could survive. But I did; I'm still here.

It has taken me 14 months to translate my experiences, thoughts, and feelings into words on paper, but in truth, it has taken me a lifetime to write this book. I wouldn't take back a single moment of any of the journey of my life. It has made me who I am. What a magnificent experience in its entirety.

This part of my process, this book, is nearly complete. There is one chapter left. But I know there is still learning and growth to come.

CHAPTER 21

COLLATERAL BEAUTY
PART 2

*Maybe my experiences, the traumas, the perceived monsters, were
really, in essence, just my Judas. A necessary force, action or betrayal
to fulfill and provide a path or destination to my own
enlightenment and evolution.*

~Audra Rene Weeks

Collateral beauty. We talked about this earlier. Collateral
beauty is the idea that even the worst situations and horrifying events can show us something beautiful. It might not
be immediately evident, but it will come to the fore. We will see it in
ourselves.

Collateral beauty gives us the opportunity to see how strong we
are, to see what we can overcome. It calls us to rise above, to levels we
otherwise may have never even known we could reach.

Events and other people's actions don't get to dictate who we are.
We have a choice of who we want to become in spite of what has happened to us. It has taken me every moment of my life to be who I am
right now. And I think I am pretty damn incredible. Who would I be

in this moment had I not experienced every single moment prior to this one?

Everything I have been through has taught me how to have more love, understanding, kindness, compassion, patience, and empathy for people, including myself. If you have ever experienced a person who lacks any of these attributes, you know it can be an unpleasant experience. So, I am grateful to have strengthened these attributes in myself as a result of what I've been through.

I have also honed my ability to connect with others on a much deeper level than someone who hasn't been through some serious shit. I have no idea what the inner workings of a non-traumatized person looks like, but I know that my inner workings are very deep, indeed.

My experiences have helped my soul and my humanity to grow and evolve. I have experienced so much light because I have experienced so much darkness. I had the choice to either dwell on what happened to me or move through it and rise above it. I choose the latter. Some days I am angry at that which I have to rise above, and some days I am astonished at how far I have risen.

⌒

I have been on an incredible journey that most will never take. My experiences have given me the opportunity to write a book and share this journey with others. Mountains can be moved; I am a living breathing example of that.

And that friends, is what I call collateral beauty.

I turned my back to darkness for so long,
pretending it wasn't there.
Always running away from the stranger
I saw in my reflection.

One day I could no longer take it,
so I decided to turn around.
I looked at my pain and said,
You're here.
You aren't leaving,
so let's make something beautiful out of you.

~Hannah Blum

My deepest gratitude to you for taking a walk through my journey. My ultimate hope is that I may shed some light onto your own path. Maybe it has given you some hope in your dark places. We are all in this together, and together we rise. Never be ashamed of who you are, what you are going through, or what you have been through. You are amazing and have so much to offer this world.

You are most definitely a hero!

ABOUT THE AUTHOR

*A*udra is a true Arizona native. She grew up in the heart of Phoenix. Belonging to a large family, she was the youngest of six children. In her adolescent years, she was an athlete involved in soccer, softball, gymnastics, and ballet. She studied psychology, philosophy, world religions, and criminal profiling in college. She later received her clinical certification in hypnotherapy as well as her certification as a Reiki Master. Audra is currently a professional nanny and a holistic healer. She is the doting mother to three children and Ommi to four grandchildren.

Audra has experienced several traumas in her life that left her with PTSD, traumatic response, and trauma patterning. She recently embarked on a healing journey through cognitive reframing therapy. Through this successful journey and her follow-up work, Audra has come to understand that trauma can be treated and even healed. She has made it her mission to share her story, and she hopes to bring hope and help to those who are navigating the pain that their own traumatic experiences have brought them.

Audra has stepped firmly onto the path of helping others and continues to put herself in the arena to change lives. She can frequently be found as a guest and co-hosting on a variety of self-exploration podcasts and live talks.

www.audrareneweeks.com
FB: Audra Rene Weeks @A.R.Weeks   IG: @audrareneweeks

If you resonated with this book, we would love
if you left a review!

Thank you!